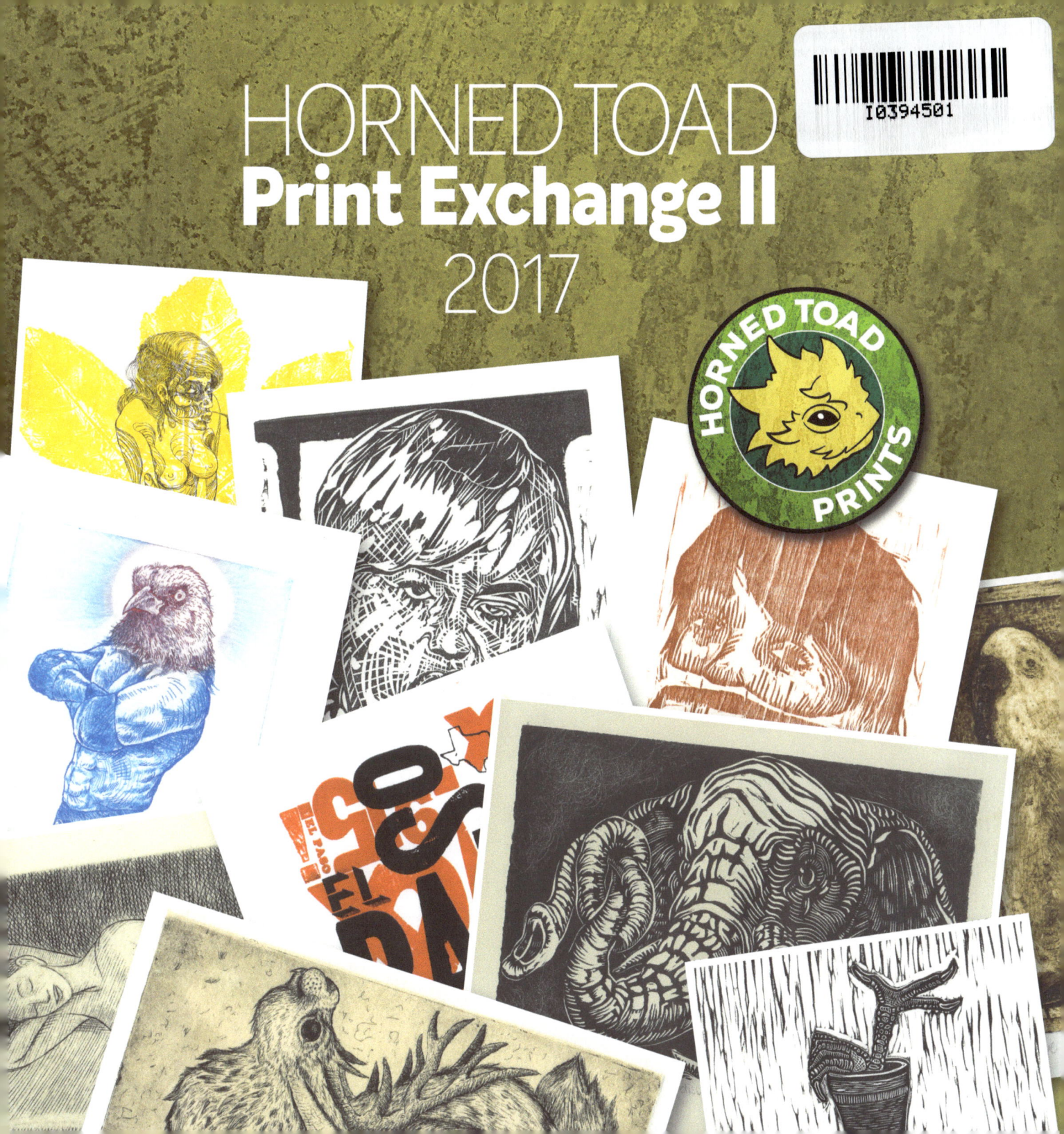

HORNED TOAD
Print Exchange II
2017

HORNED TOAD PRINTS

HORNED TOAD
Print Exchange II
2017

Manuel Guerra — Project Leader
Raul Monarrez — Project Assistant
Krrrl — Art Agitator
www.manuelguerra.net/exchange-archives.html

Introduction

In the summer of 2014 Horned Toad Prints, located in El Paso, Texas, hosted its first international print exchange. We had 28 participants in the exchange. It traveled around the country and was exhibited from 2014-2016.

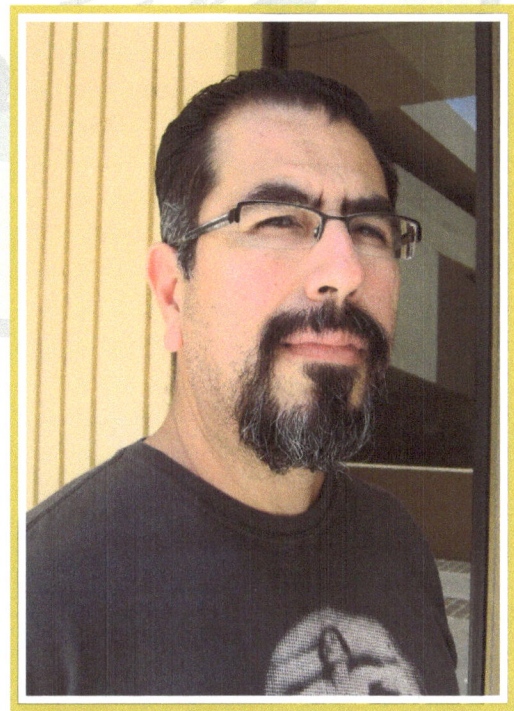

In the spring of 2016, I attended the SGCI print conference in Portland along with KRRRL, the art agitator, to promote the Desert Triangle Print Carpeta and... wow, what a site. A homecoming event. Prints and printmakers everywhere. The vibe felt good! It was through this experience and some brews that I decided to announce the Horned Toad Prints Second Print Exchange this past fall.

This second Horned Toad Print Exchange was open themed, where printmakers worldwide were invited to submit an edition of 10, original, hand-pulled prints using any of the following techniques: Intaglio, Lithography, Relief, and Serigraphy. The participants receive 8 randomly selected prints from the exchange, and the remaining two prints are archived at The Horned Toad Prints studio and used for exhibition. In addition, a print exchange is a great way for printmakers to trade prints, build their personal art collection, and exhibit side by side with other artists of different levels.

There are 53 artists sharing their work in this year's exchange. We are happy to present them here to you in this catalog. Enjoy!

Manuel Guerra — 2017

PRINT EXCHANGE II **ARTISTS**

Pavel **Acevedo**
"Mascara"
Relief Print
Riverside, California USA

Miguel **Aguilar**
"Welcome"
Relief Print
El Paso, Texas USA

Adrian **Aguirre**
Intaglio
Villa de Zaachila, Oaxaca
Mexico

Christin **Apodaca**
Serigraph
El Paso, Texas USA

David **Barista**
"Bet On The Bay"
Serigraph
Decatur, Illinois USA

Aaron **Bass**
"Sailing The Seas of Destiny"
Intaglio
Albuquerque, New Mexico USA

Louise **Beauchamp**
"Ginko II "
Relief Print
Stroud, Gloucestershire UK

Laurie D. **Brown**
"Snake"
Relief Print
Seattle, Washington USA

Glenn **Buack**
"Sultan Akbar's Tour of India"
Drypoint
Tucson, Arizona USA

Ashley B. **Cranney**
"Craneo Pintado"
Mixed Media Print
Phoenix, Arizona USA

Diane **Davis**
"Chacala Muse"
Intaglio
Seattle, Washington USA

Aaron **deGruyter**
Serigraph
Las Cruces, New Mexico USA

Francisco **Delgado**
"El Discurso"
Relief Print
El Paso, Texas USA

Maria **Doering**
"Authenticity"
Relief Print
Dartmouth, Nova Scotia
Canada

Hector Josue **Felix** Martinez
Collograph
Villa de Zaachila, Oaxaca
Mexico

Miguel **Flores**
"Aguas Por El Tiempo"
Relief Print
Riverside, California USA

Jules **Floss**
"Shaman"
HIPs Engraving
Yuma, Arizona USA

Sam **Garcia**
"You're Not Always With Me"
Relief Print
El Paso, Texas USA

Susan "Skuishi" **Gonzalez**
"Pain Killer"
Relief Print
El Paso, Texas USA

Cameron **Gray**
"Presidents Day"
Serigraph
St. Louis, Missouri USA

Manuel **Guerra**
"El Vals Entre La Mano
Pachona Y El Diablito"
Serigraph
El Paso, Texas USA

Eric **Hodgins**
"Angel of Burns"
Intaglio
Phoenix, Arizona USA

Brian **Lane**
"Dissonance"
Serigraph
Auburn, Washington USA

Eli **Levin**
"Sleeping Girl"
Engraving
Dixon, New Mexico USA

Abby **Mattison**
"Coyote Realizes Her Dream"
Intaglio
Dixon, New Mexico USA

Alberto Fabricio **Melchor** Diaz
Intaglio
Villa de Zaachila, Oaxaca
Mexico

Jorge **Mendoza** Garcia
Collograph
Villa de Zaachila, Oaxaca
Mexico

David **Mohallatee**
"0305201"
Mixed Media
Richmond, Kentucky USA

Raul **Monarrez**
"Estas Como Un Pajarito
Muerto"
Relief Print
El Paso, Texas USA

Giana **Montero**
"Cloud On A Sunny Day"
Serigraph
Atherton, California USA

Juan de Dios **Mora**
"I'm Chulo"
Intaglio
San Antonio, Texas USA

Gustavo **Mora** Perez
"Carroceria"
Relief Print
Oakland, California USA

Henry **Morales**
"Nude"
Relief Print
Albuquerque, New Mexico
USA

Deena **Mustin**
"El Paso Y Que"
Letterpress
El Paso, Texas USA

Lyn **Nicholls**
"I've Seen A Cockatoo"
Collograph
Riddells Creek, Victoria
Australia

Gabriel Luis **Perez**
"Tear That Cherry Out"
Relief Print
Las Cruces, New Mexico
USA

Jorge "Yorch" **Perez**
"Tiro De Gracia"
Serigraph
Ciudad Juarez, Chihuahua
Mexico

Krittika **Ramanujan**
"Lyinching- Bridge #7"
Serigraph
Albuquerque, New Mexico
USA

Beatriz A. **Rivas** Palacios
Mixed Media
Villa de Zaachila, Oaxaca
Mexico

Augustine **Romero**
"Cuauhtemoc"
Relief Print
Albuquerque, New Mexico
USA

Humberto **Saenz**
"Gallo"
Relief Print
San Antonio, Texas USA

Marco **Sanchez**
"Santa Fe Bridge"
Relief Print
El Paso, Texas USA

Alan **Serna**
"Libre Y Luchando"
Lithograph
Lexington, Kentucky USA

Ashley **Shaul**
"Unlucky"
Intaglio
Eastpointe, Michigan USA

Ryan **Stander**
"Memories Converge"
Aquatint
Minot, North Dakota USA

Ralph **Steeds**
"Spectors"
Lithograph
Red Springs, North Carolina
USA

Lorna **Turner**
"Third + North Colorado"
Serigraph
Santa Monica, California
USA

Andrea **Velasquez**
Drypoint/Monoprint
Villa de Zaachila, Oaxaca
Mexico

Diane **Vera**
"Exaneration"
Serigraph
El Paso, Texas USA

Dania **Villanueva**
"Anaglifo"
Serigraph
El Paso, Texas USA

Georgia **Ward-Collings**
"Wolf Deck"
Serigraph
Seattle, Washington USA

Jim **Weaver**
"The Wolf's Dog"
Relief Print
Ada, Oklahoma USA

Karl "Krrrl" **Whitaker**
"Dreaming Conejos"
Serigraph
Albuquerque, New Mexico
USA

Print Exchange II
ARTIST
Locations

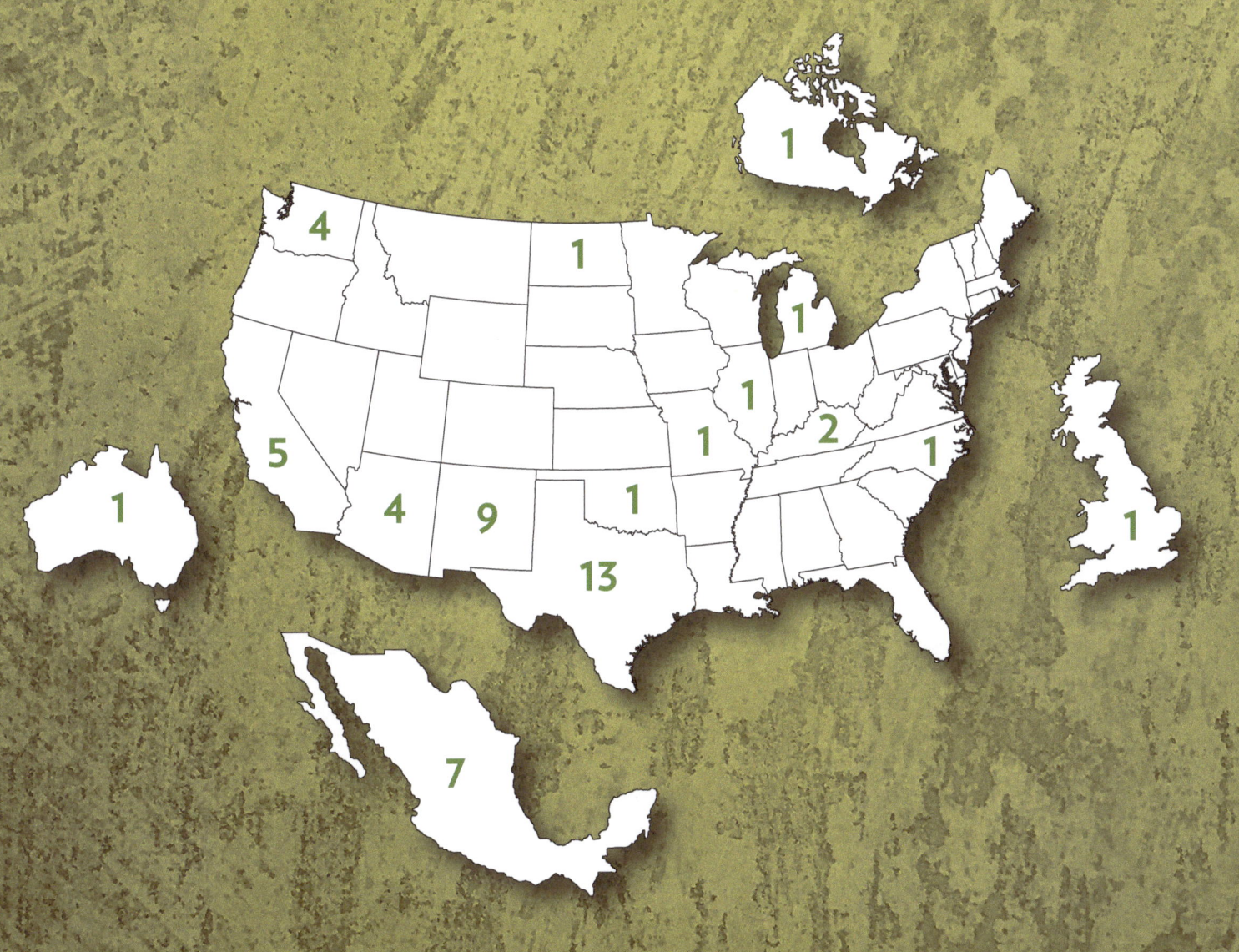

HORNED TOAD
Print Exchange II
2017

{ ALL PRINTS ARE 8 X 10 INCHES }

EXCEPT THE PAVEL ACEVEDO PRINT (8.5 X 11 INCHES)

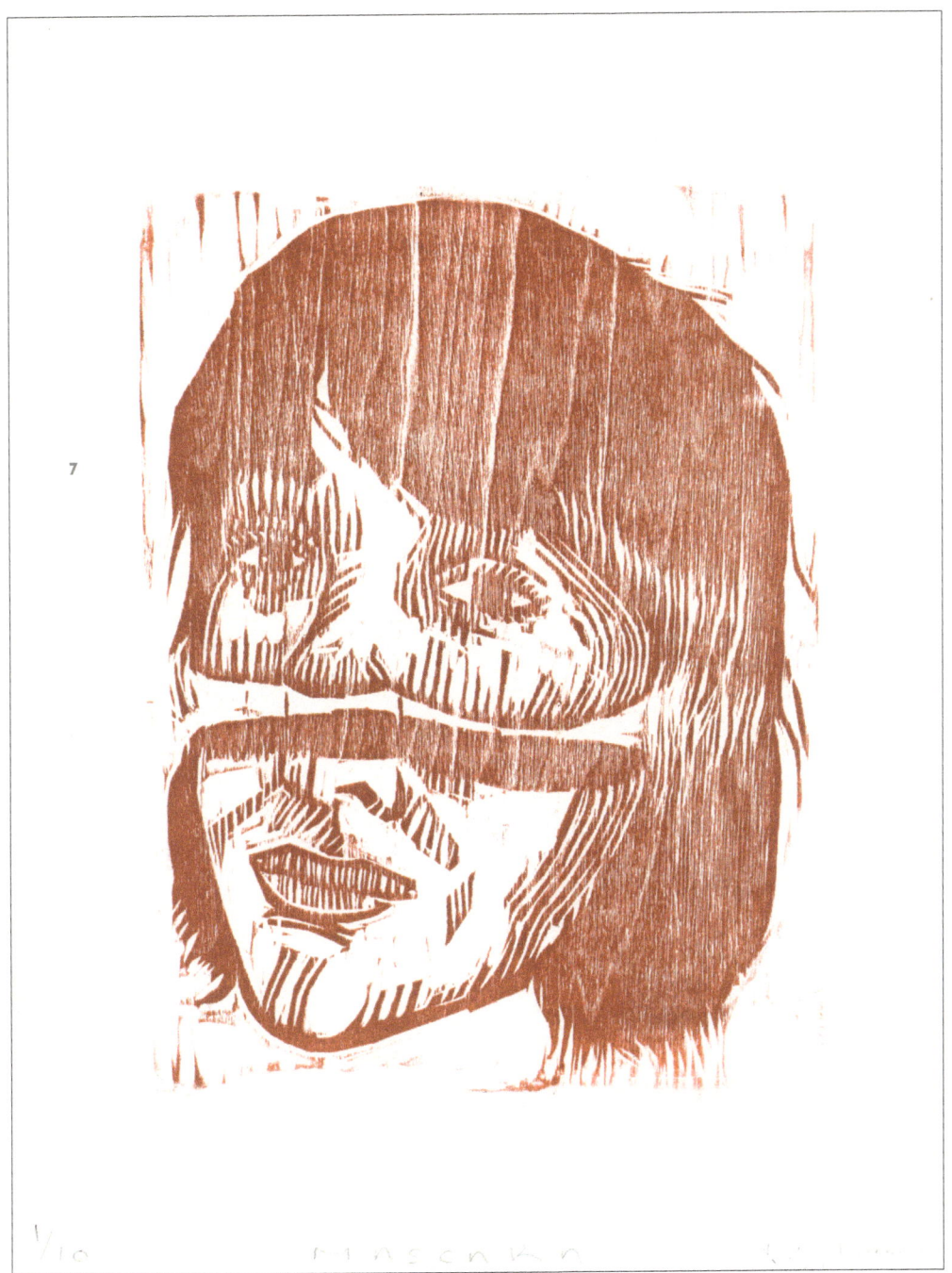

Pavel **Acevedo**
"Mascara"
Relief Print
Riverside, California USA

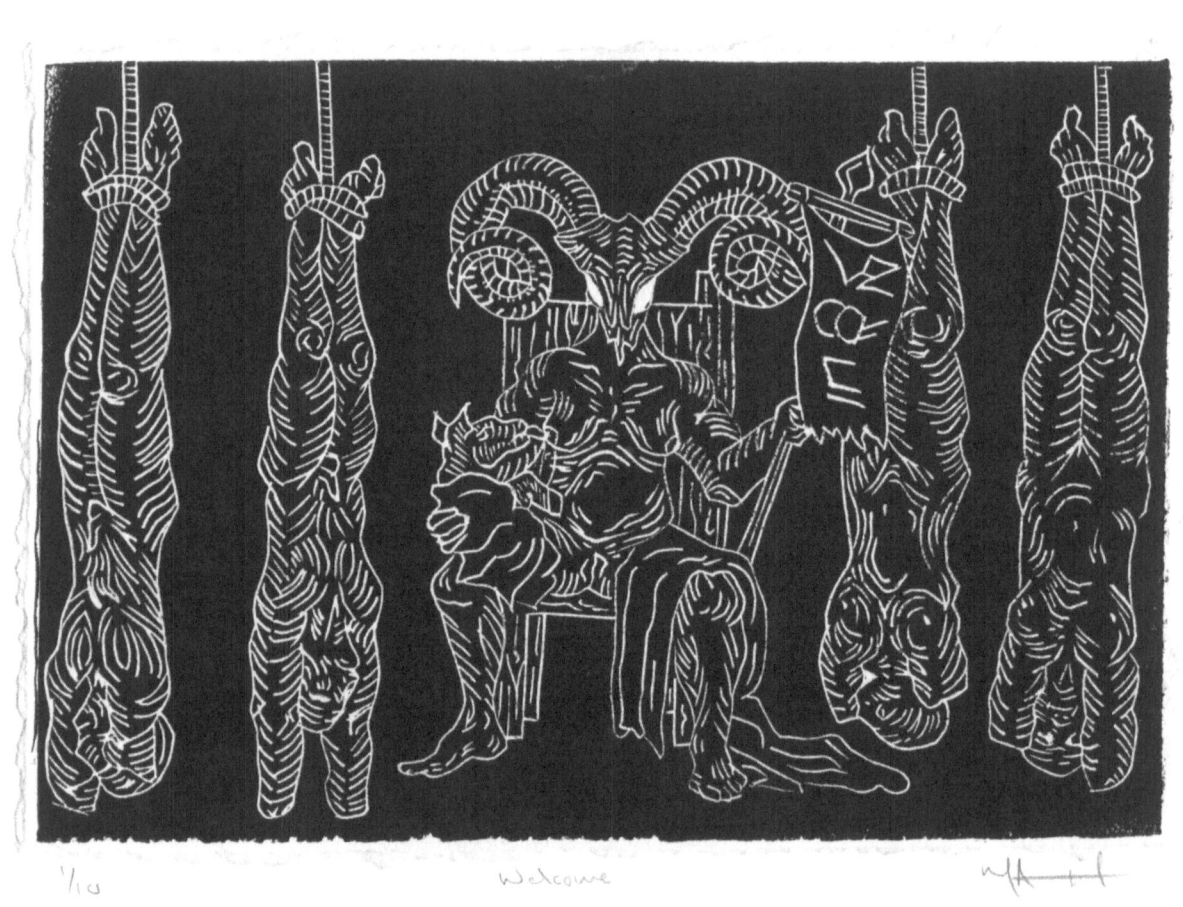

1/10   Welcome

Miguel **Aguilar**
"Welcome"
Relief Print
El Paso, Texas USA

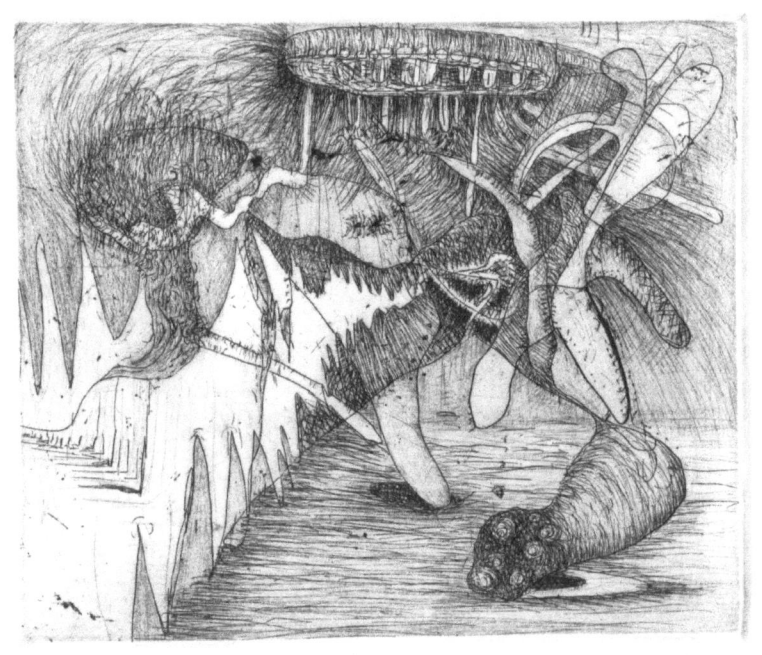

Adrian **Aguirre**
Intaglio
Villa de Zaachila, Oaxaca Mexico

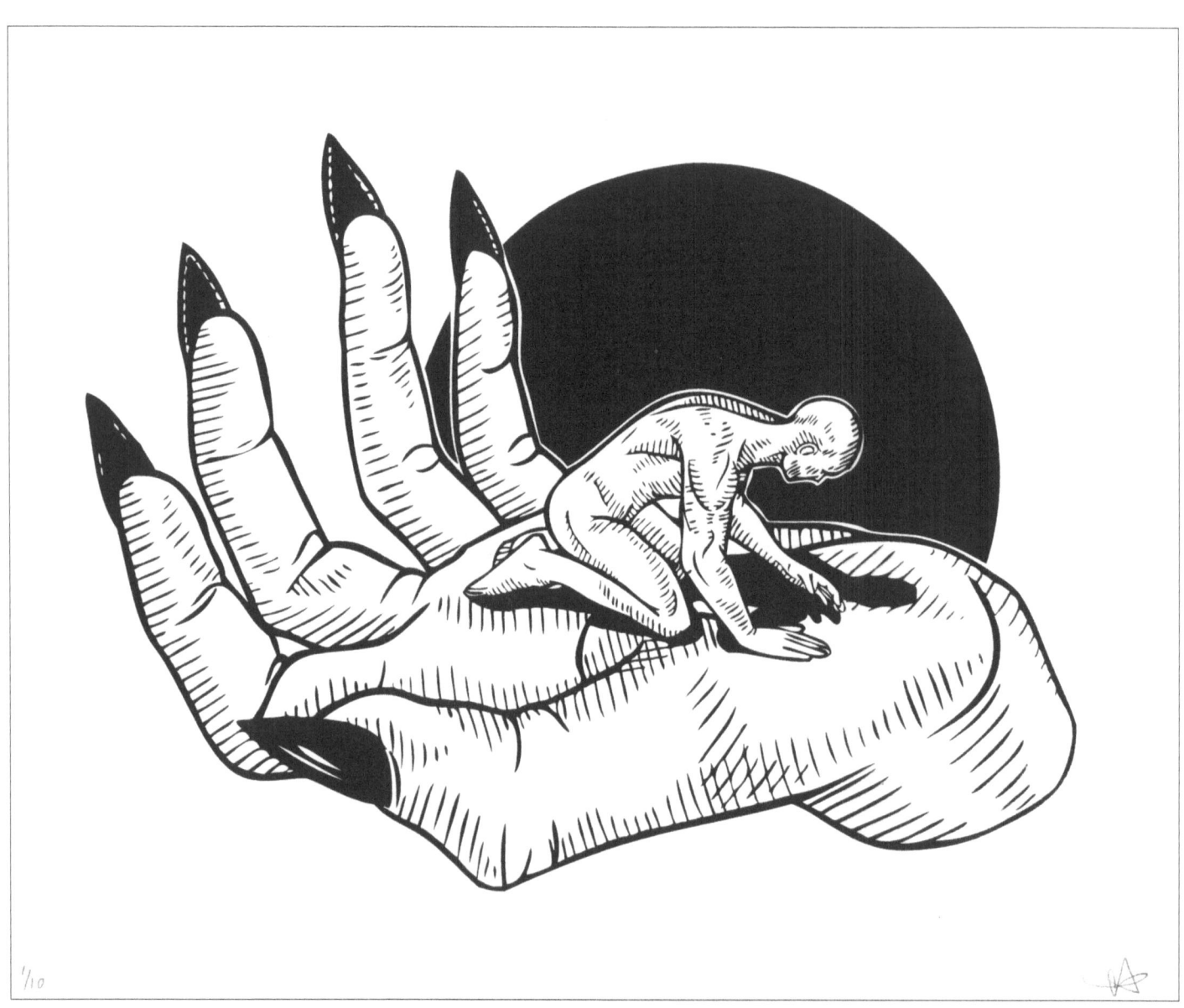

1/10

Christin **Apodaca**
Serigraph
El Paso, Texas USA

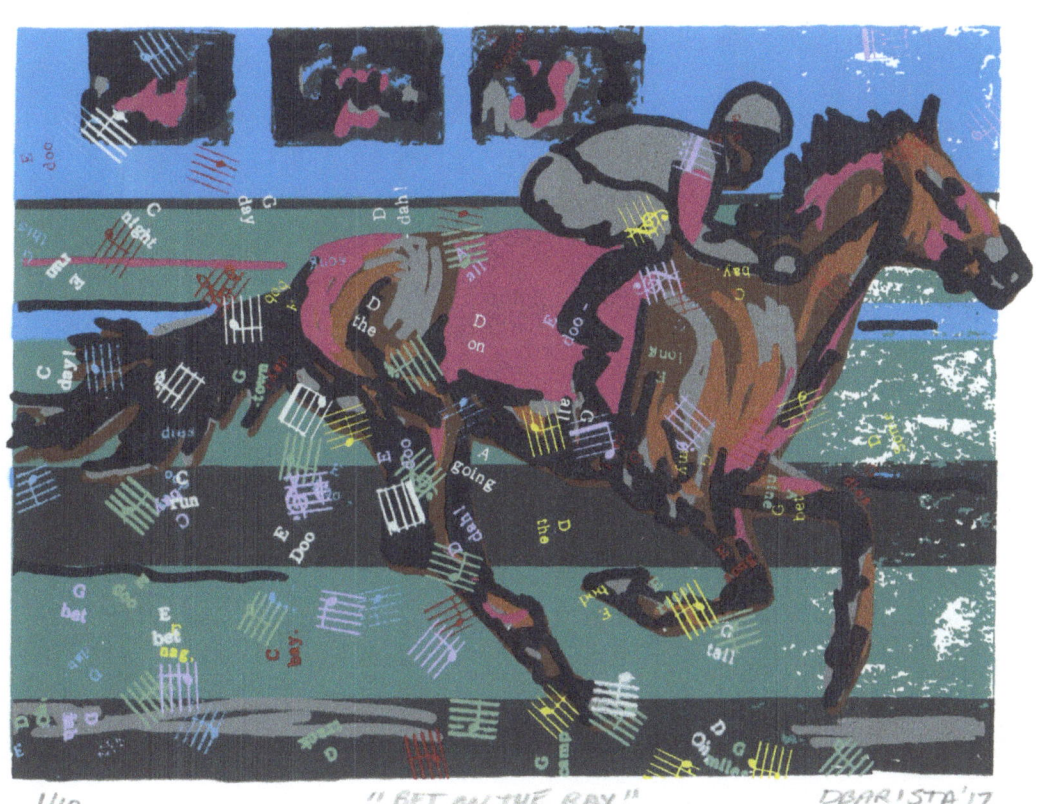

1/10   "BET ON THE BAY"   DBARISTA'17

David **Barista**
"Bet On The Bay"
Serigraph
Decatur, Illinois USA

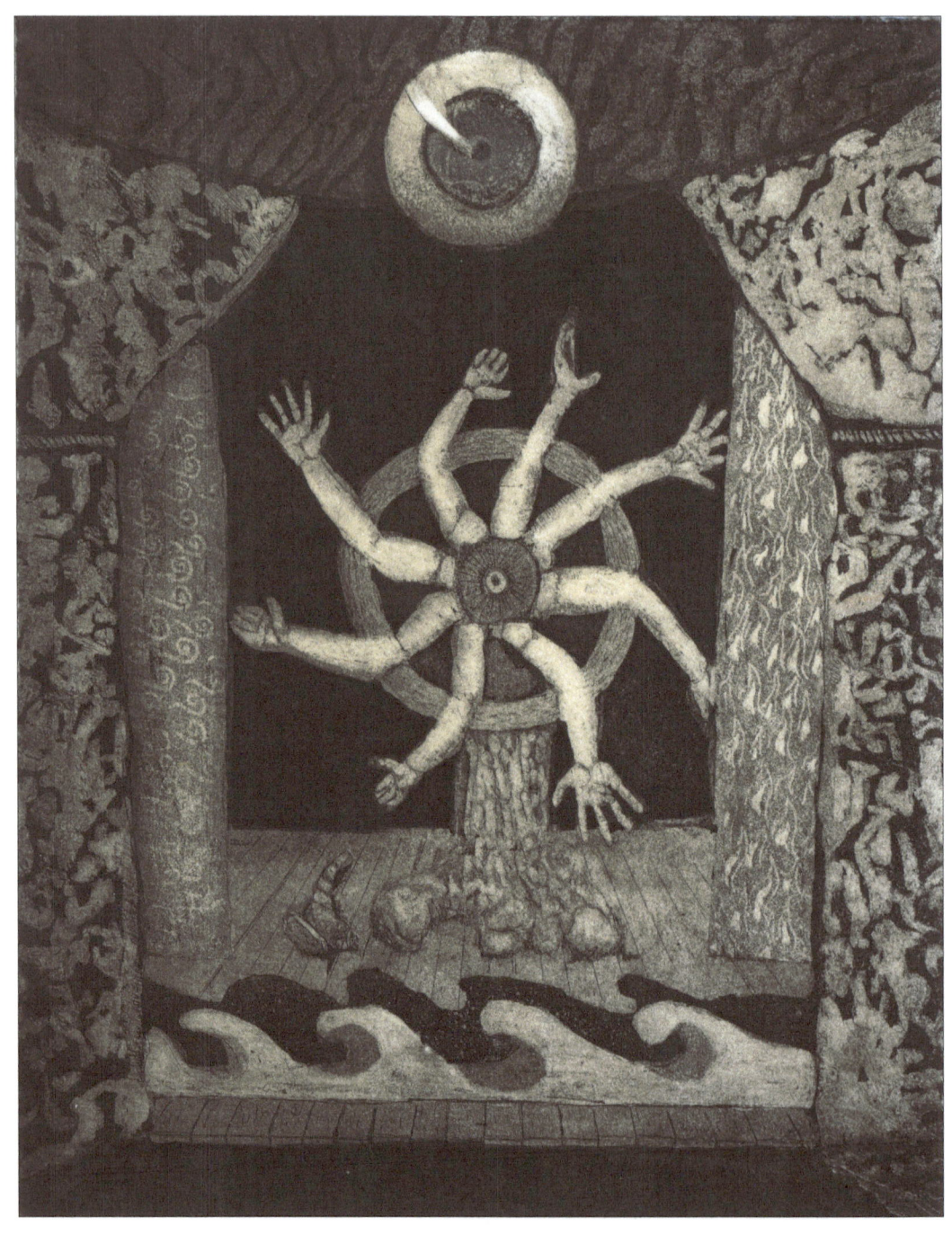

Aaron Bass
"Sailing The Seas of Destiny"
Intaglio
Albuquerque, New Mexico USA

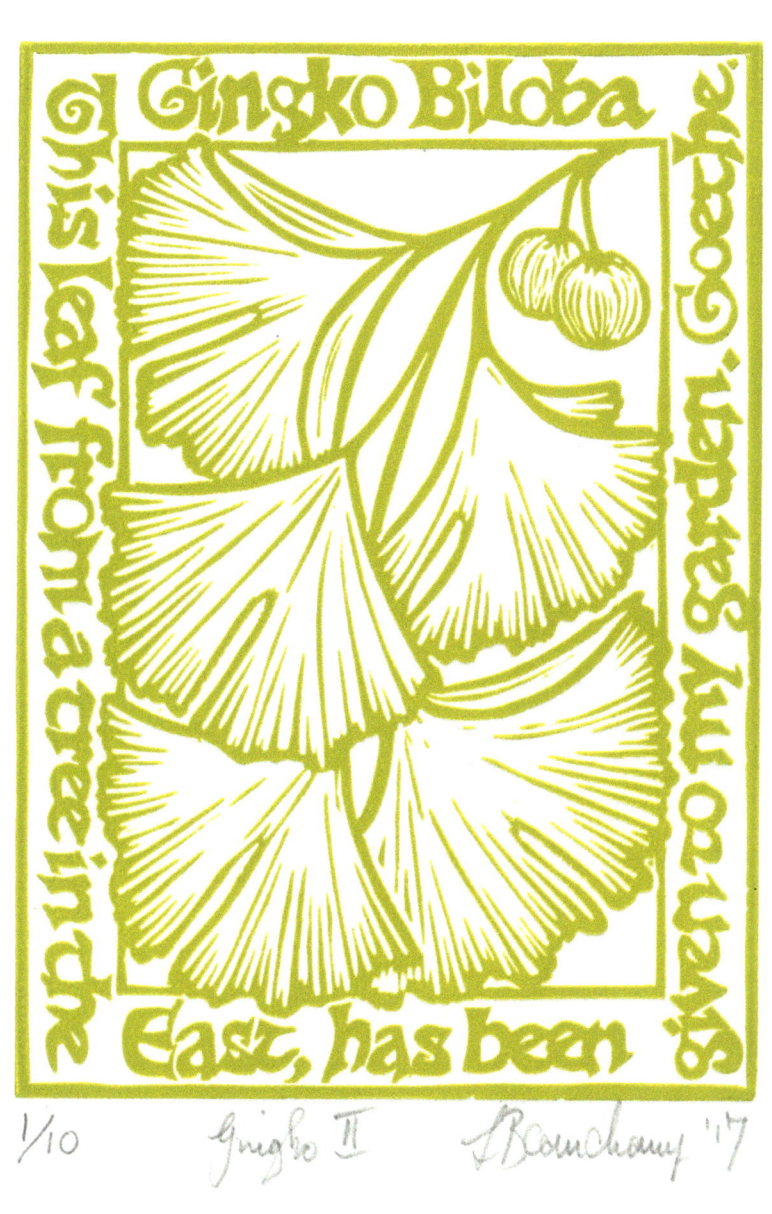

1/10   Ginkgo II   L Beauchamp '17

Louise Beauchamp
"Ginko II"
Relief Print
Stroud, Gloucestershire UK

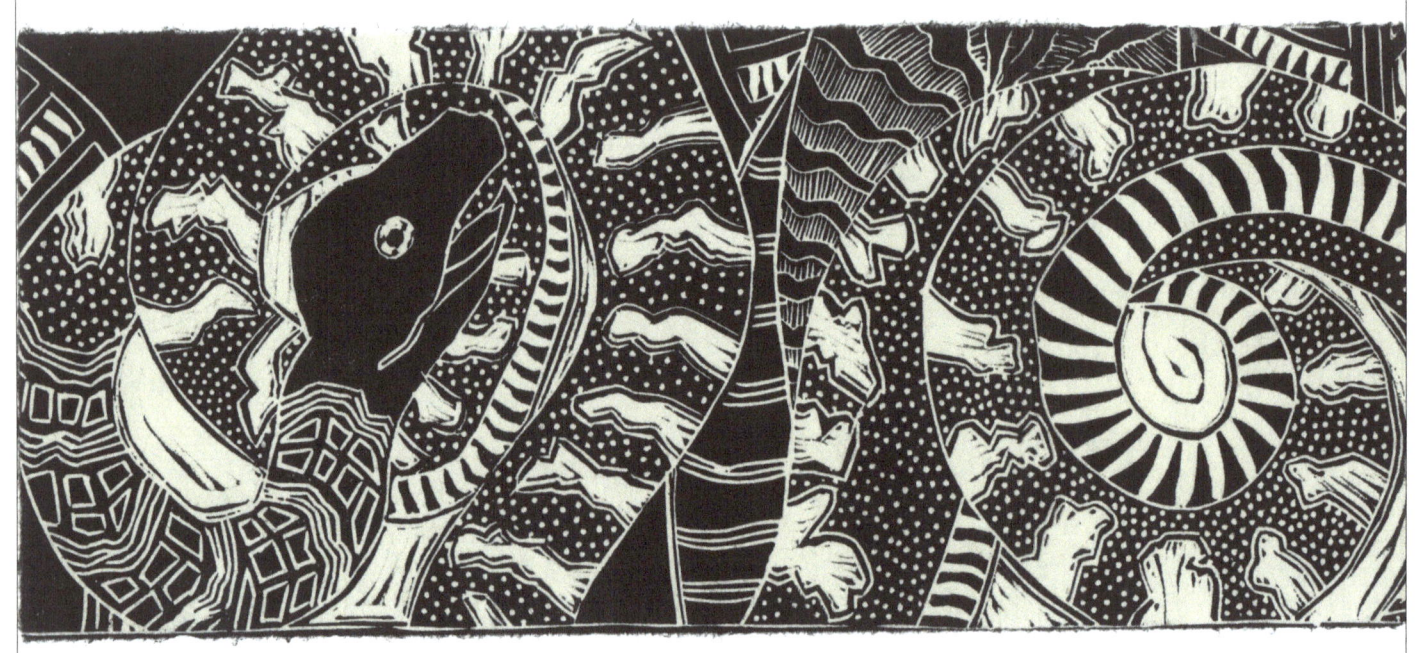

11/10   "Snake"   2017

Laurie D. **Brown**
"Snake"
Relief Print
Seattle, Washington USA

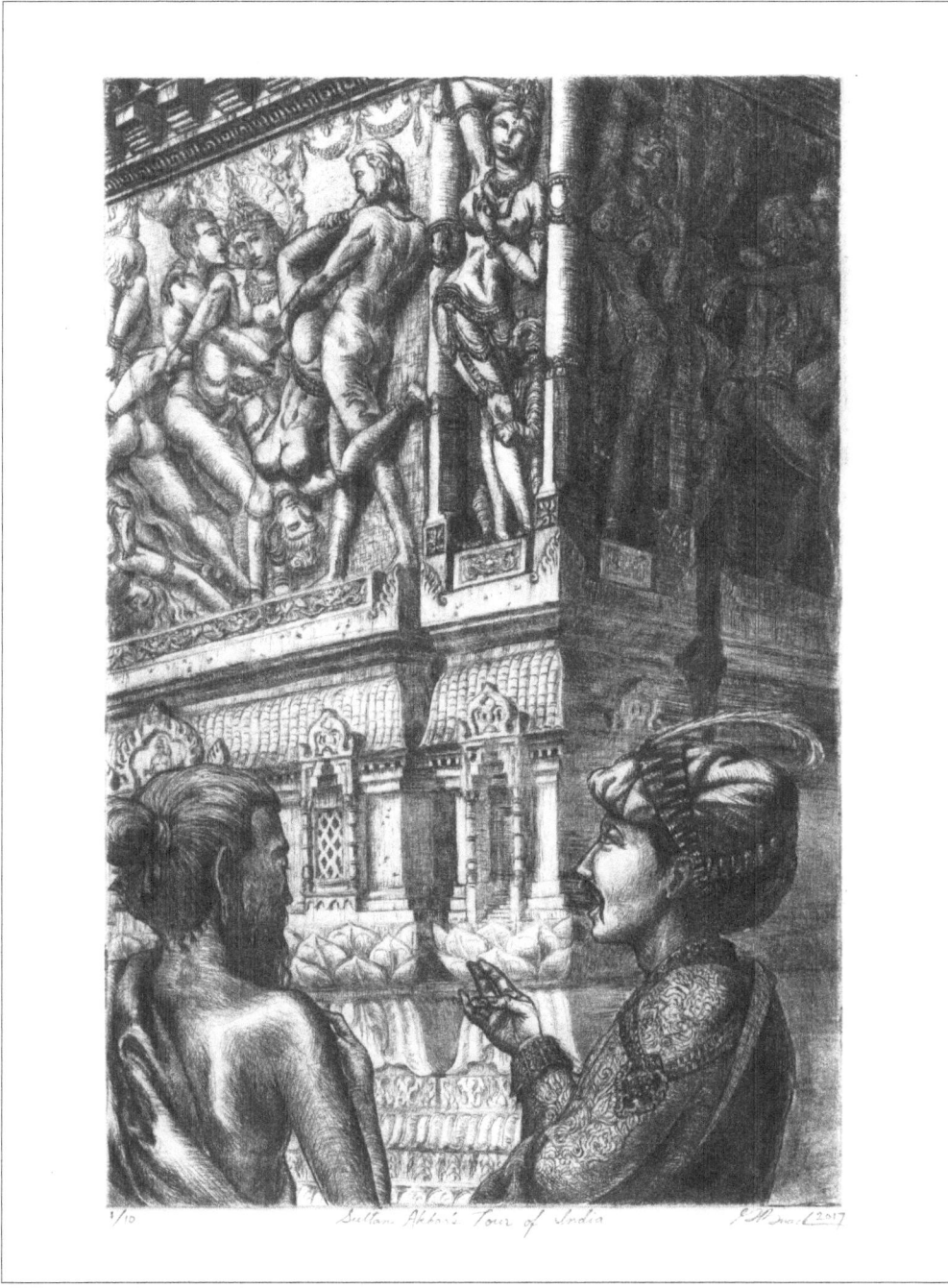

Glenn Buack
"Sultan Akbar's Tour of India"
Drypoint
Tucson, Arizona USA

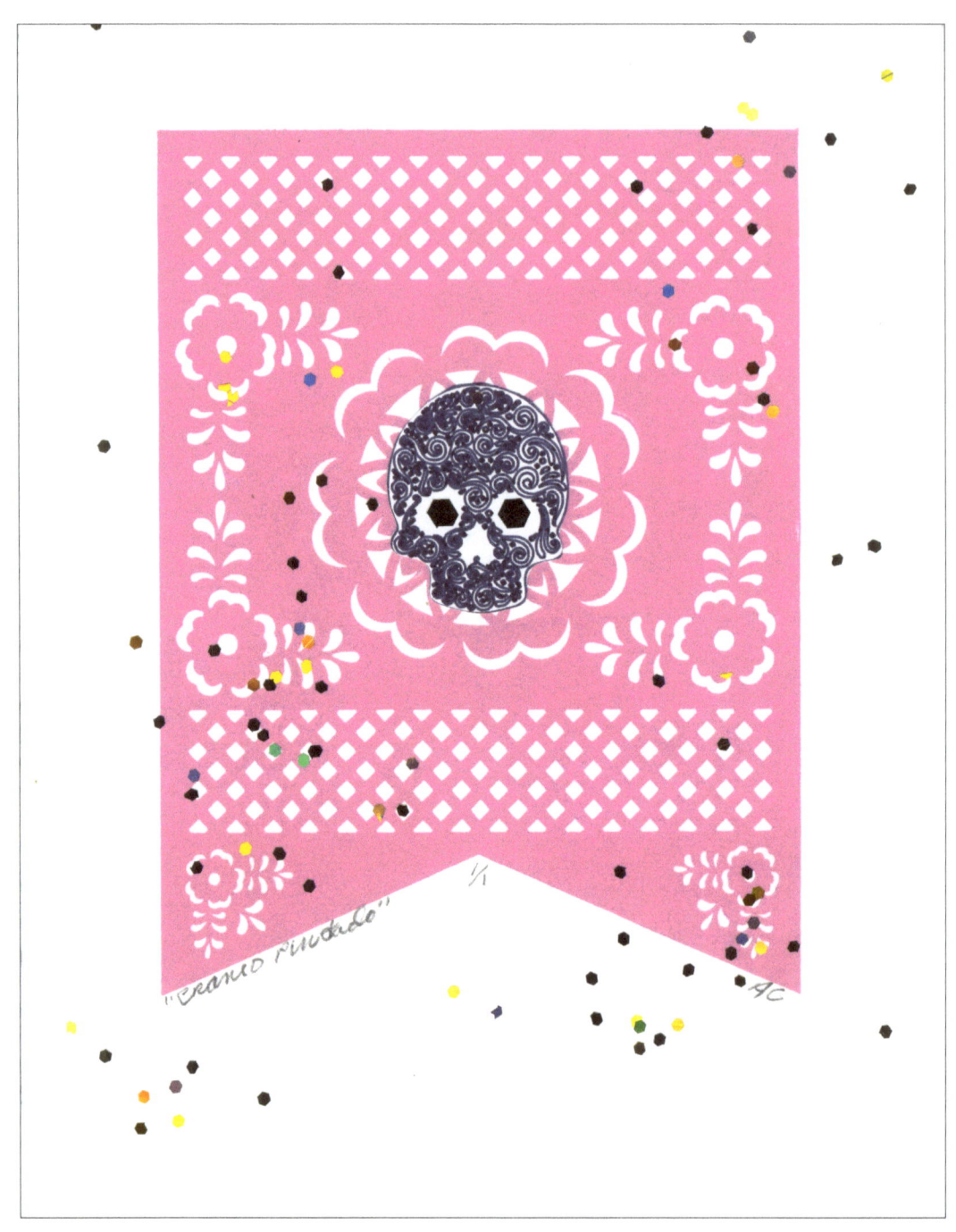

Ashley B. **Cranney**
"Craneo Pintado"
Mixed Media Print
Phoenix, Arizona USA

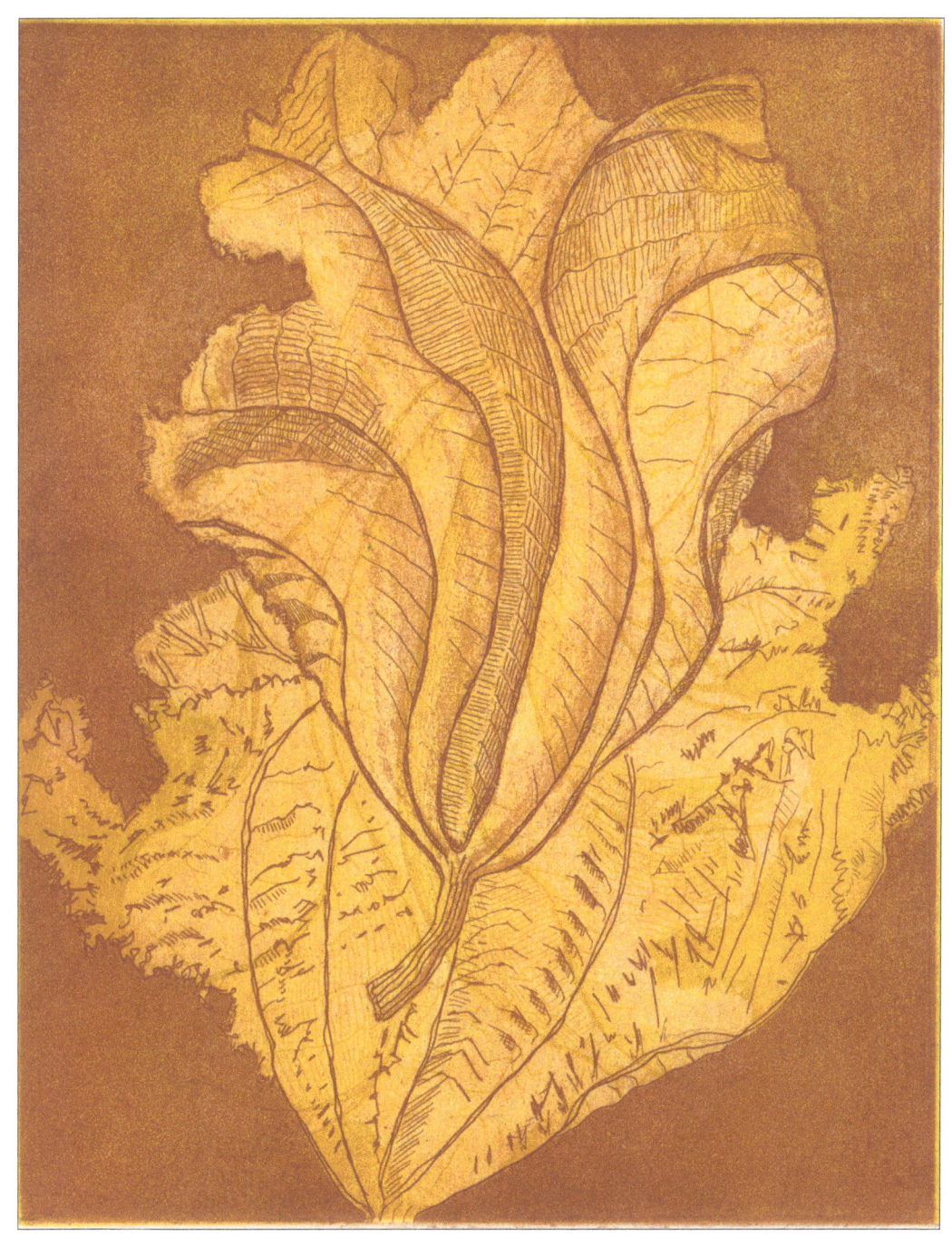

Diane **Davis**
"Chacala Muse"
Intaglio
Seattle, Washington USA

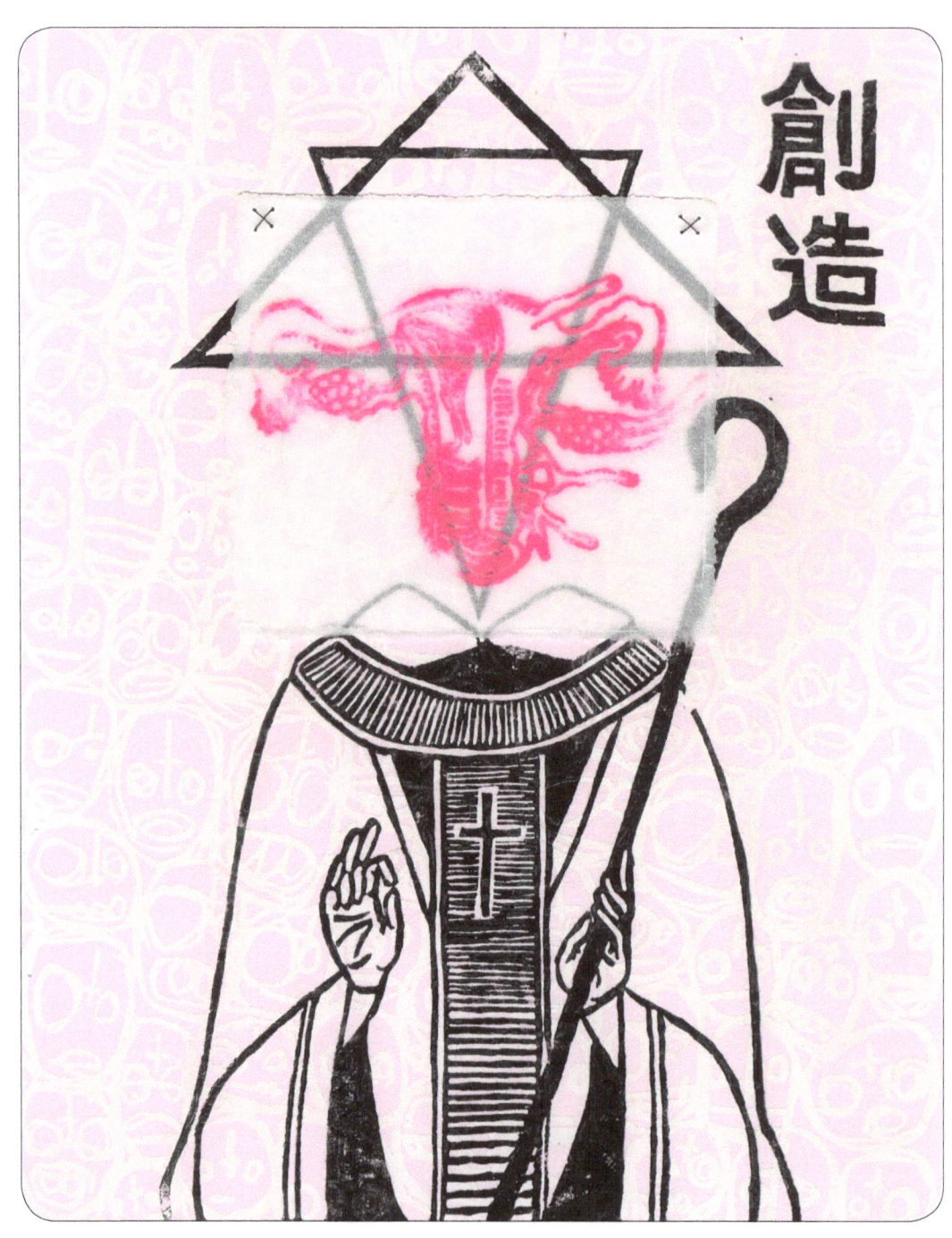

Aaron deGruyter
Serigraph
Las Cruces, New Mexico USA

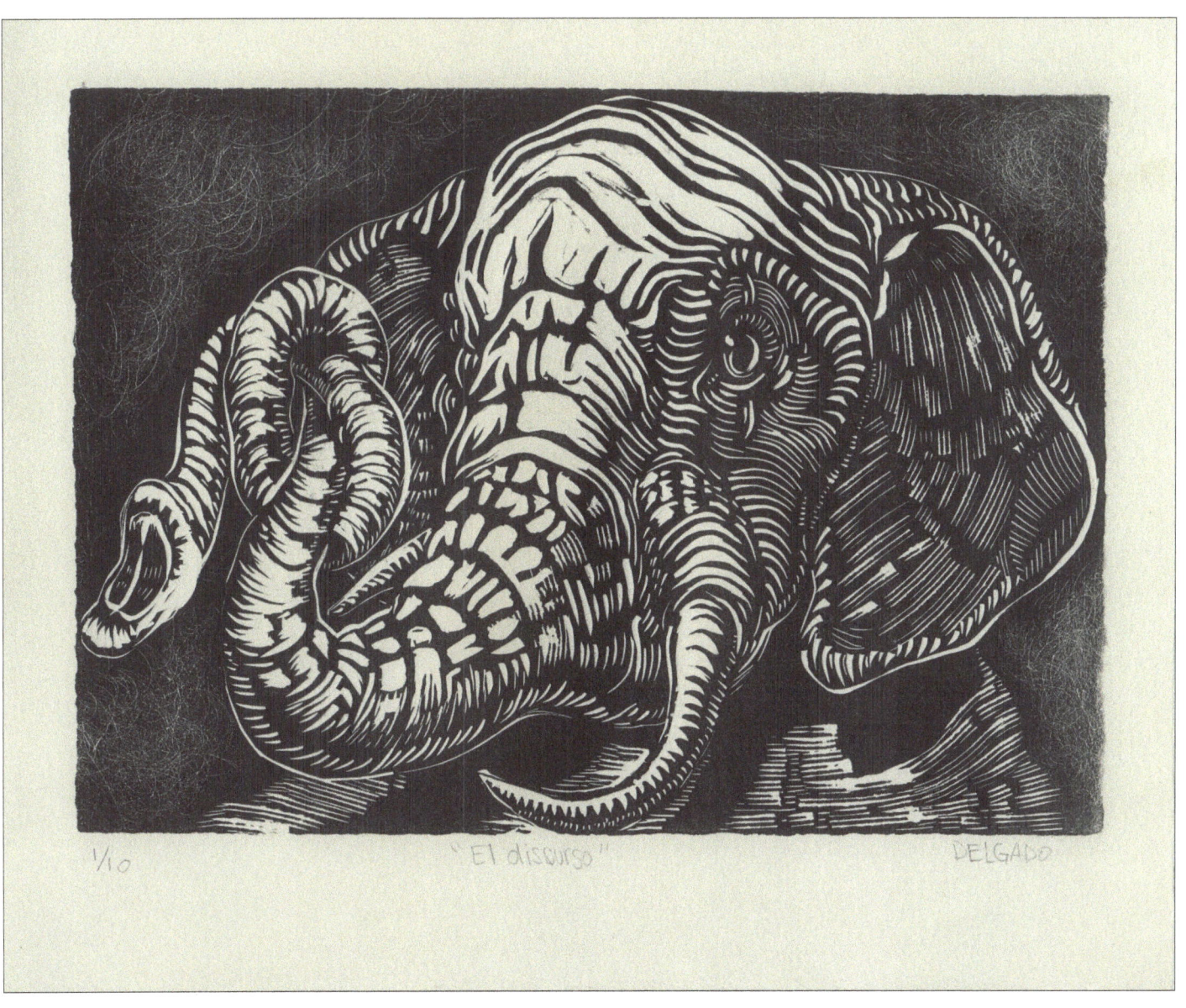

1/10   "El discurso"   DELGADO

Francisco **Delgado**
"El Discurso"
Relief Print
El Paso, Texas USA

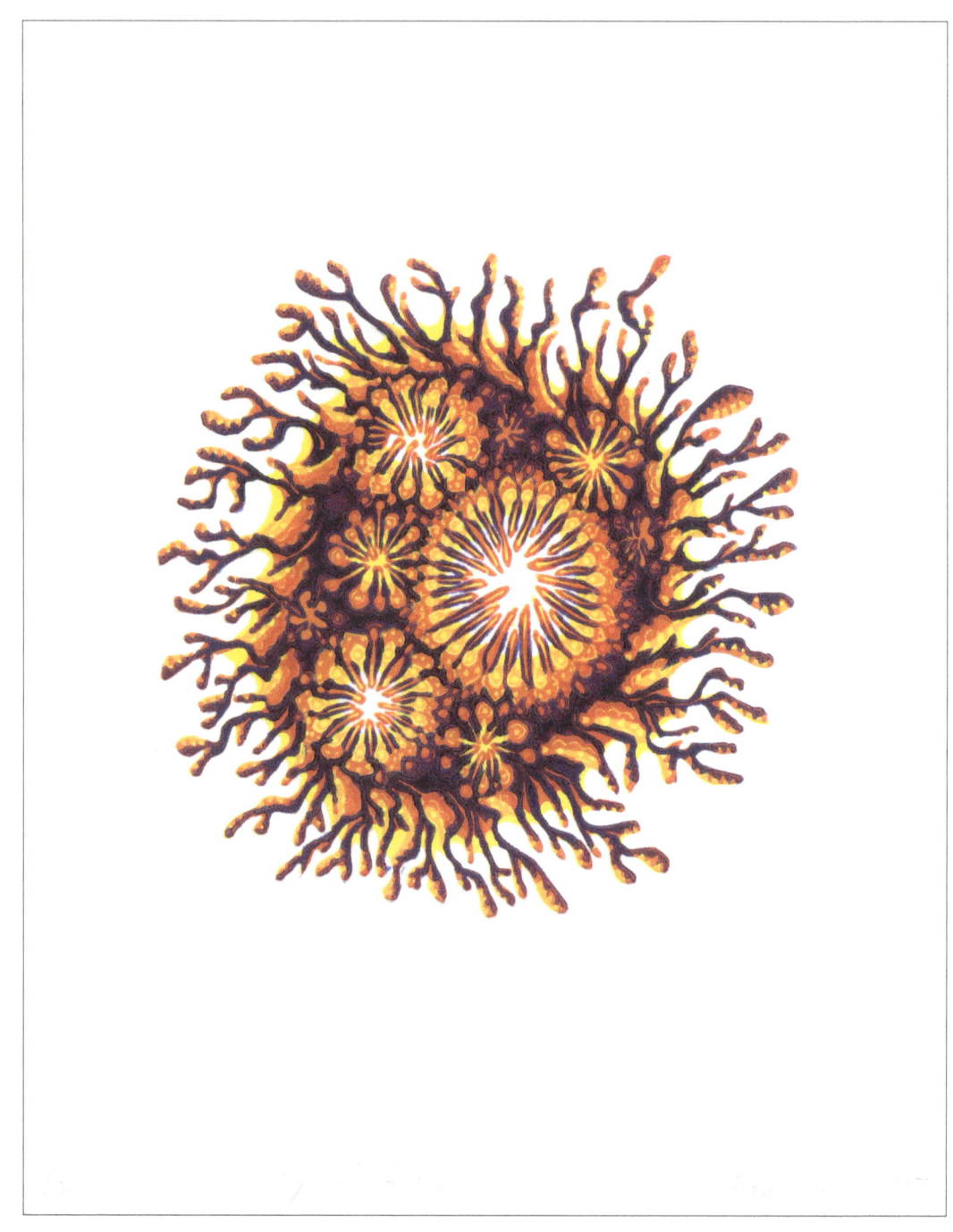

Maria **Doering**
"Authenticity"
Relief Print
Dartmouth, Nova Scotia Canada

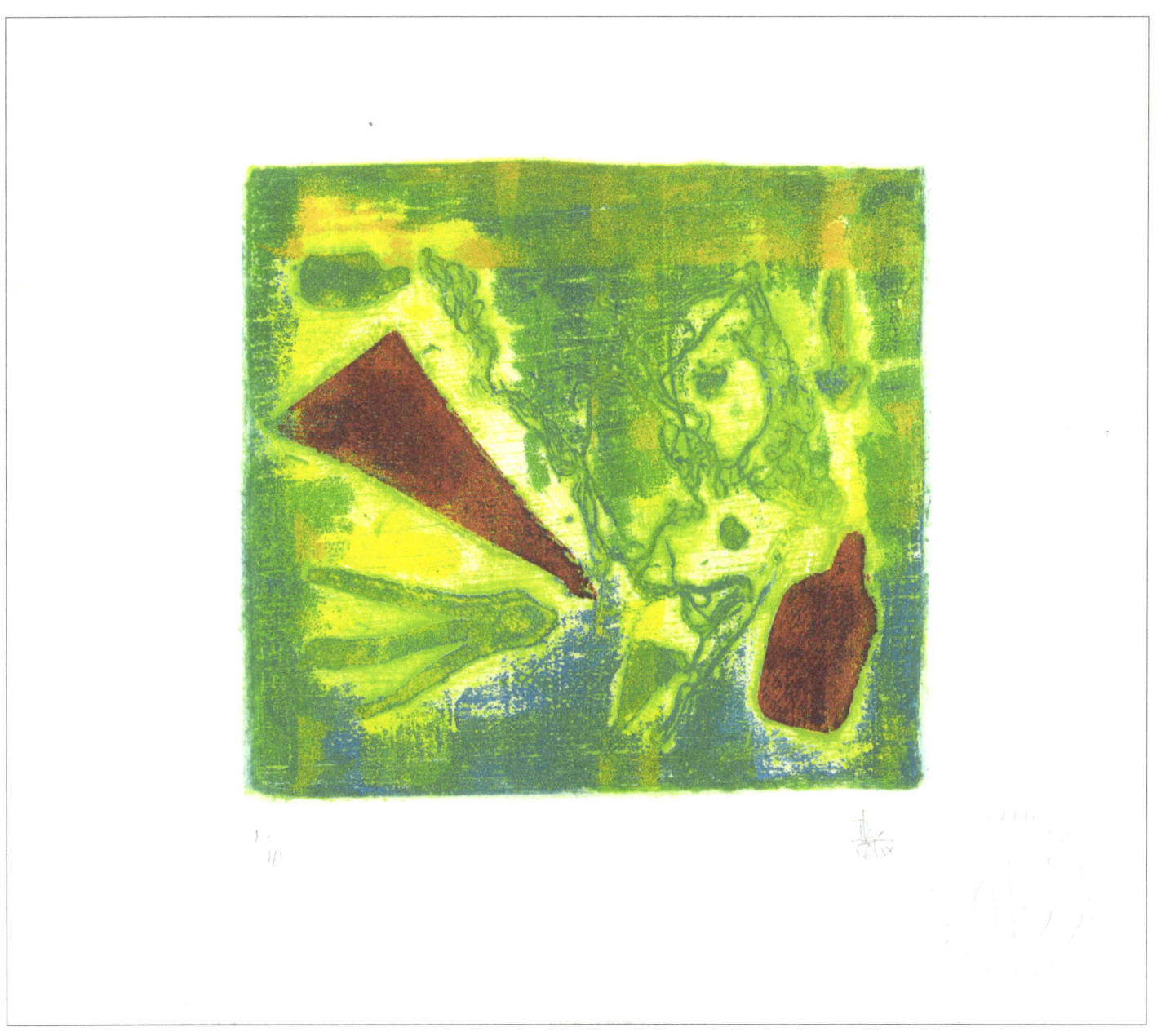

Hector Josue **Felix** Martinez
Collograph
Villa de Zaachila, Oaxaca Mexico

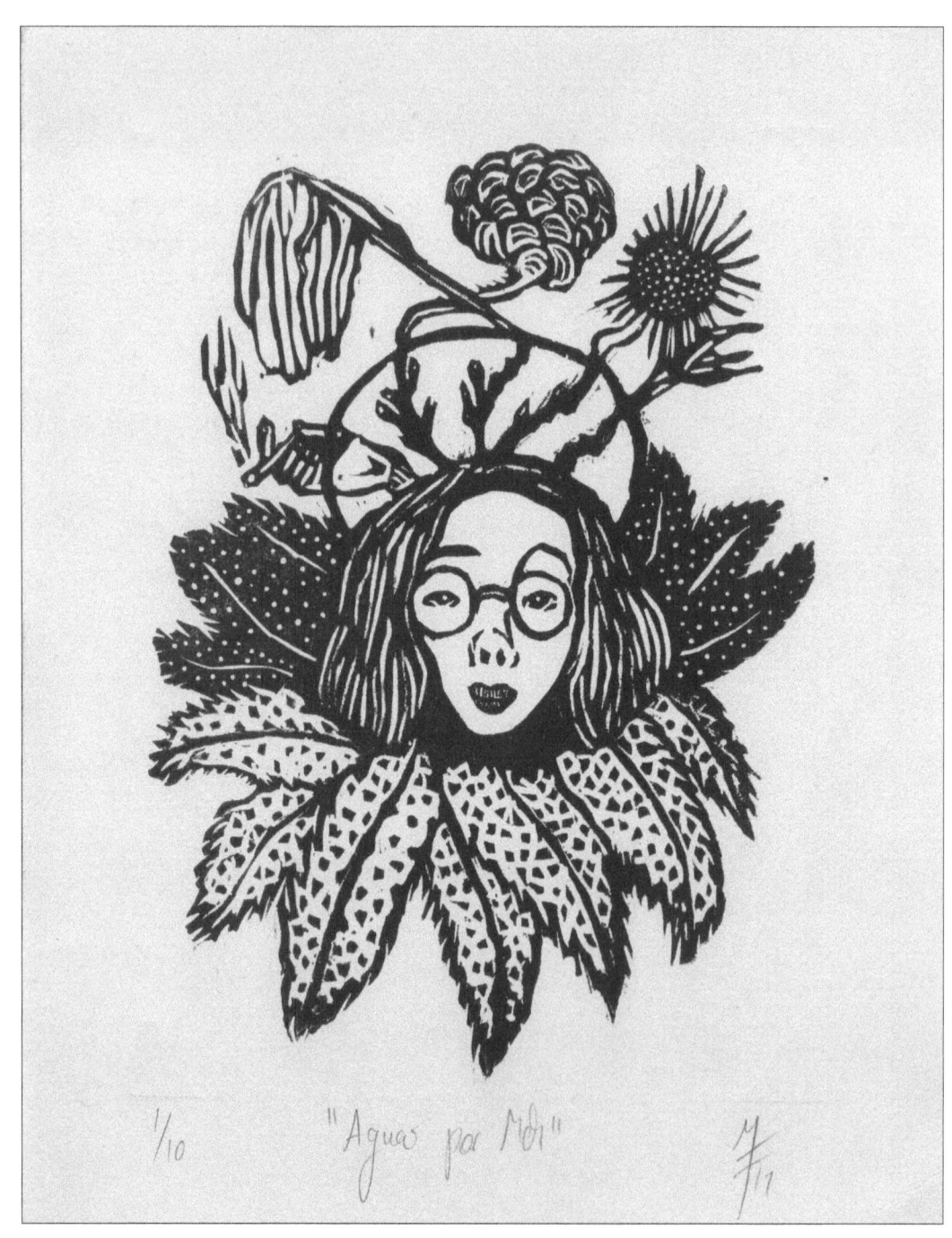

1/10   "Aguas por Má"   M 7/11

Miguel Flores
"Aguas Por El Tiempo"
Relief Print
Riverside, California USA

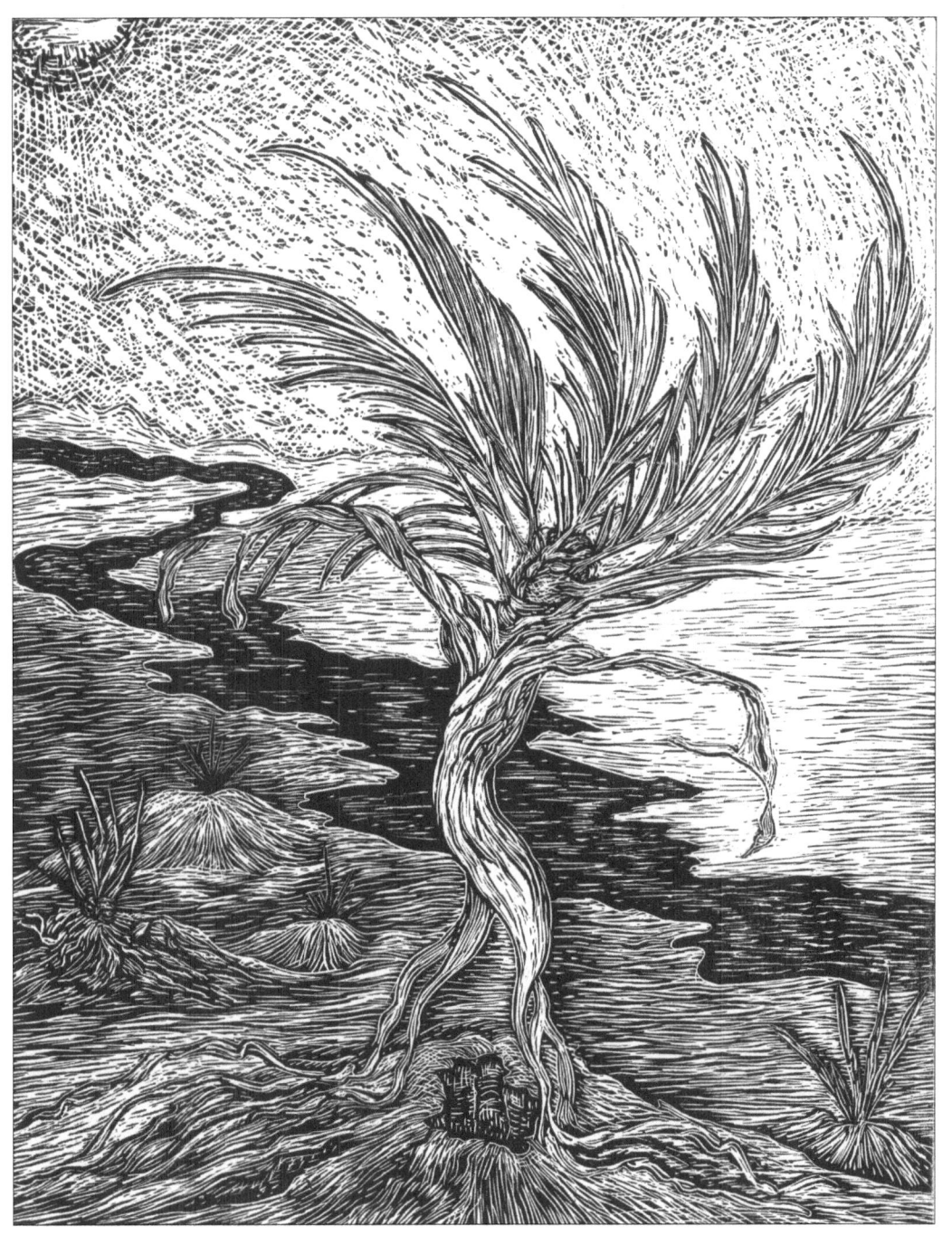

Jules **Floss**
"Shaman"
HIPs Engraving
Yuma, Arizona USA

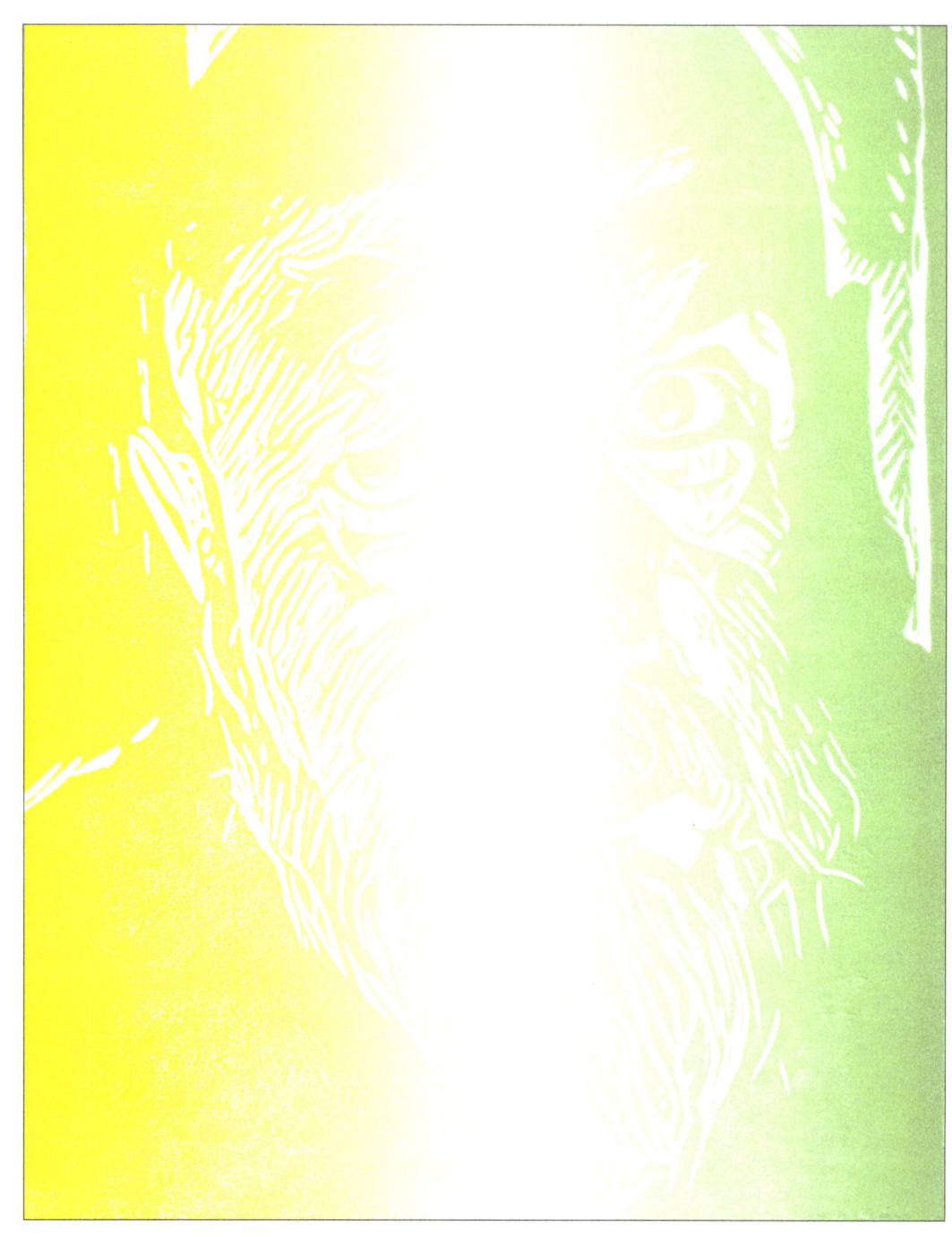

Sam **Garcia**
"You're Not Always With Me"
Relief Print
El Paso, Texas USA

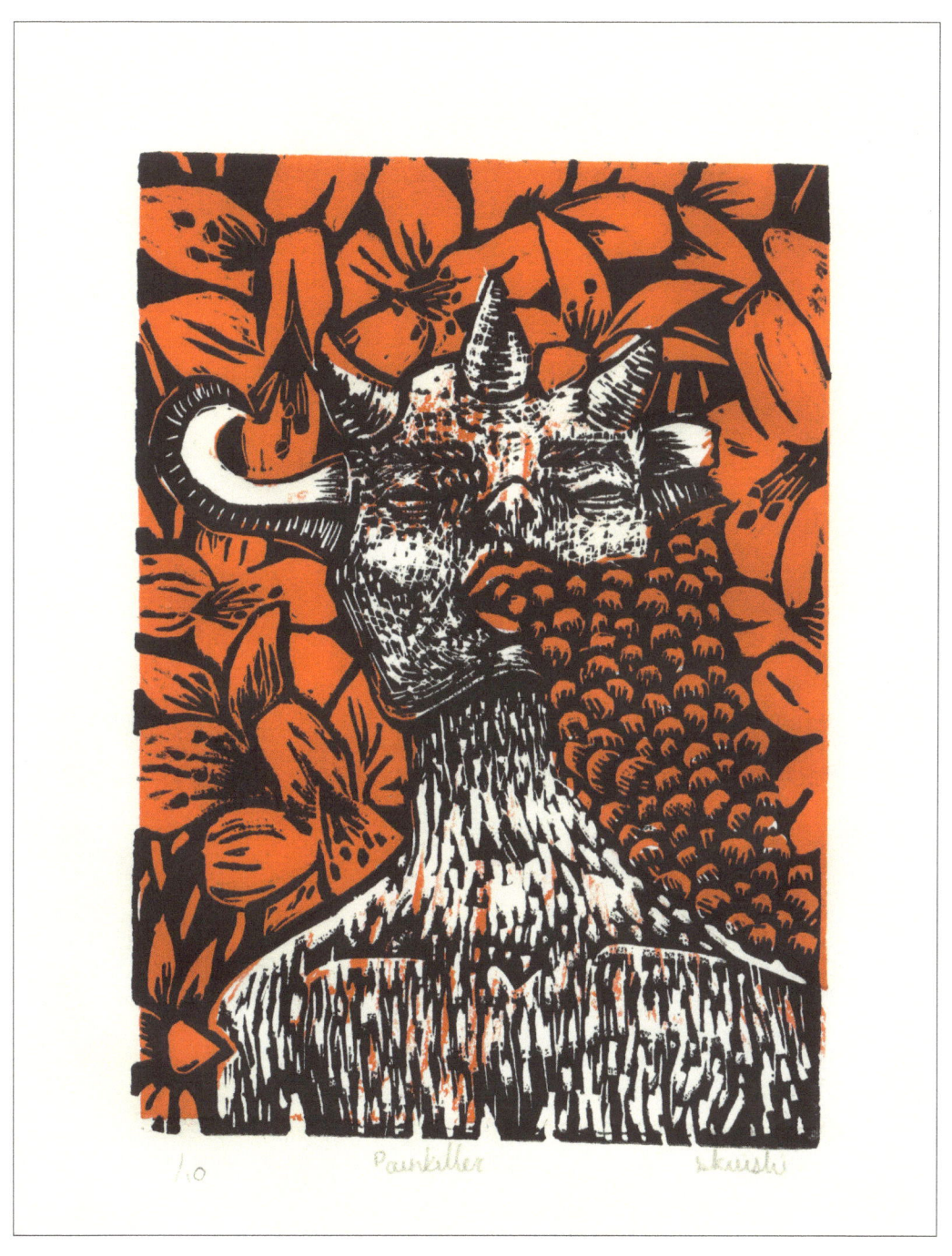

1.0   Painkiller   skuishi

Susan "Skuishi" **Gonzalez**
"Pain Killer"
Relief Print
El Paso, Texas USA

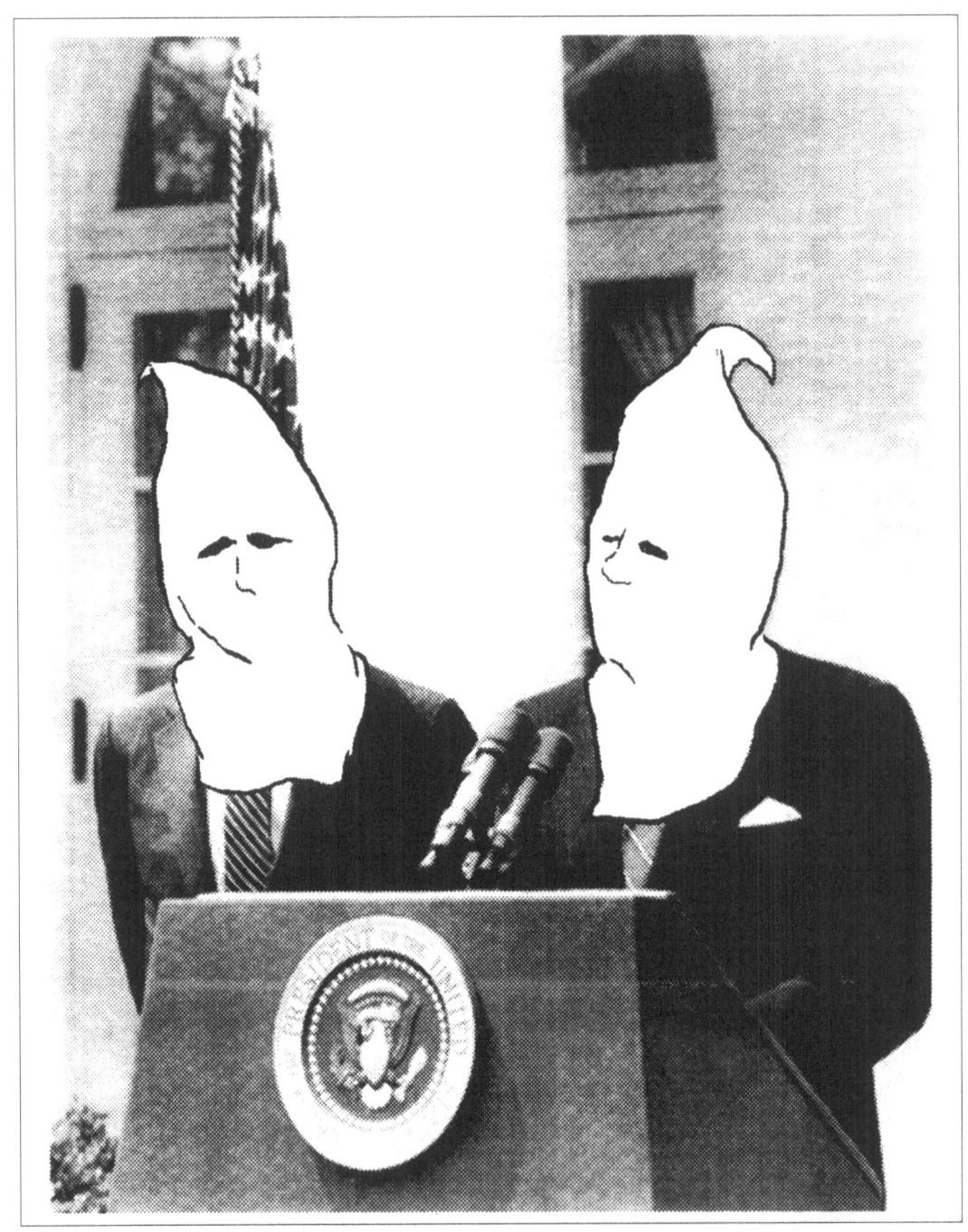

Cameron **Gray**
"Presidents Day"
Serigraph
St. Louis, Missouri USA

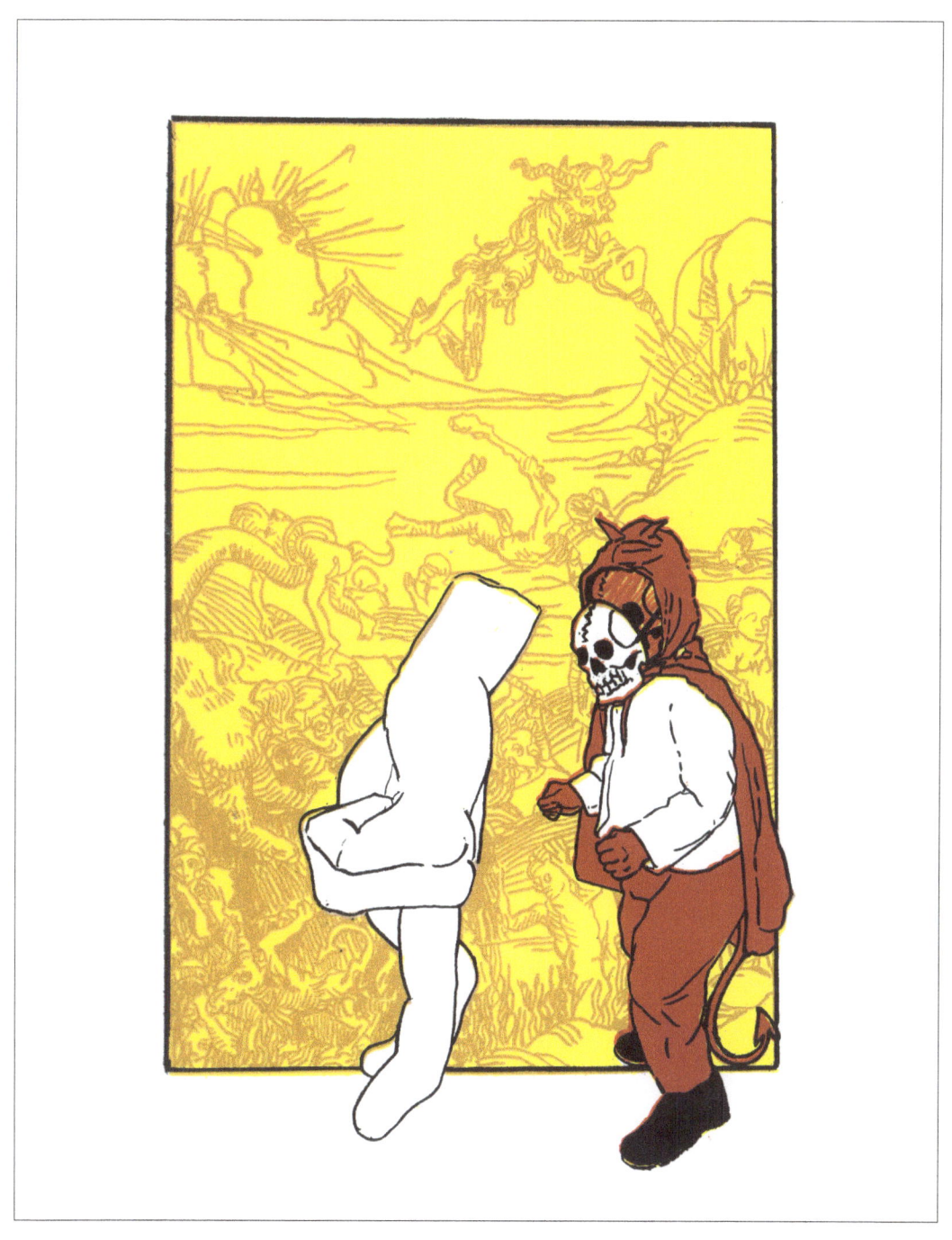

Manuel **Guerra**
"El Vals Entre La Mano Pachona Y El Diablito"
Serigraph
El Paso, Texas USA

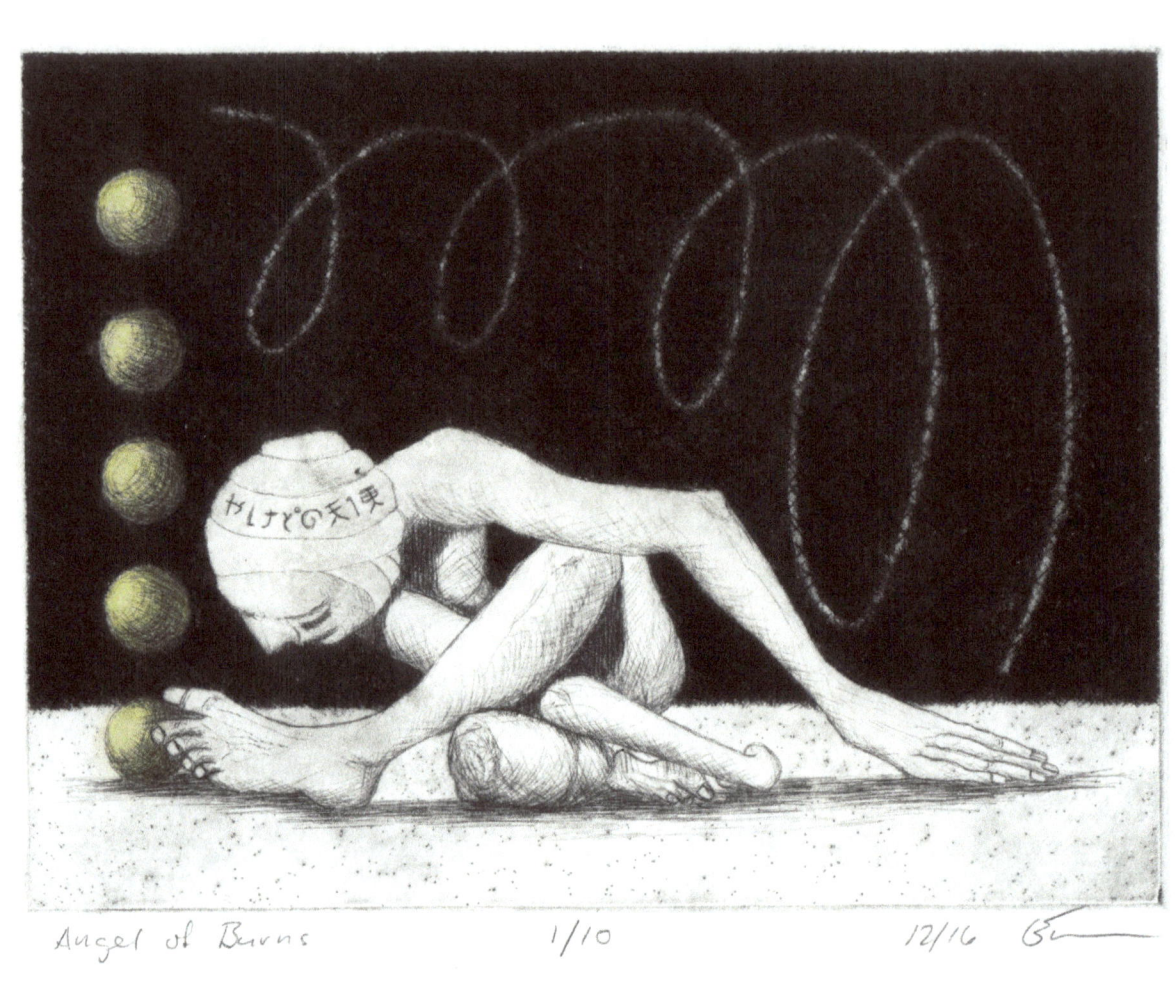

Angel of Burns   1/10   12/16

Eric Hodgins
"Angel of Burns"
Intaglio
Phoenix, Arizona USA

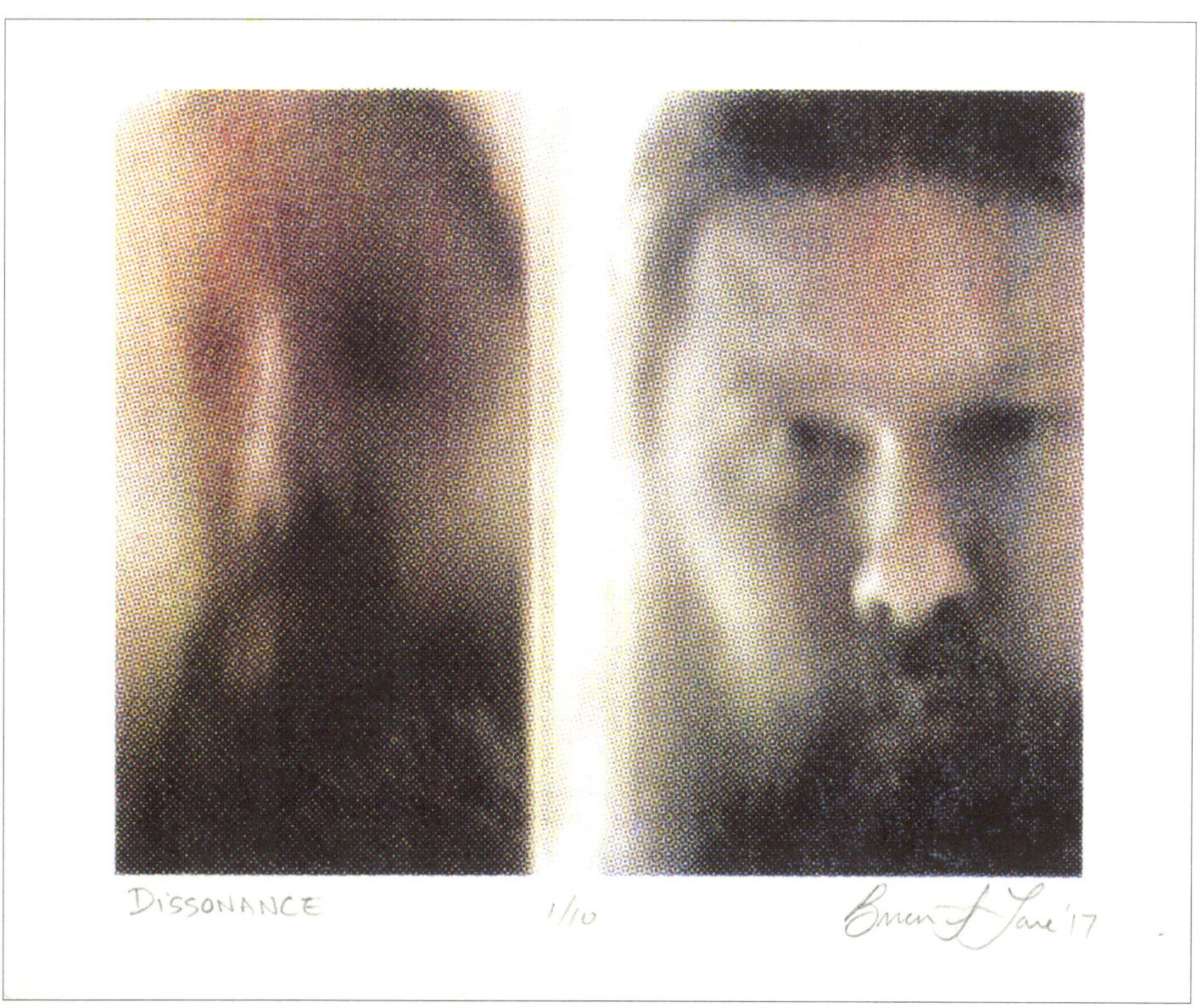

DISSONANCE   1/10   Brian Lane '17

Brian **Lane**
"Dissonance"
Serigraph
Auburn, Washington USA

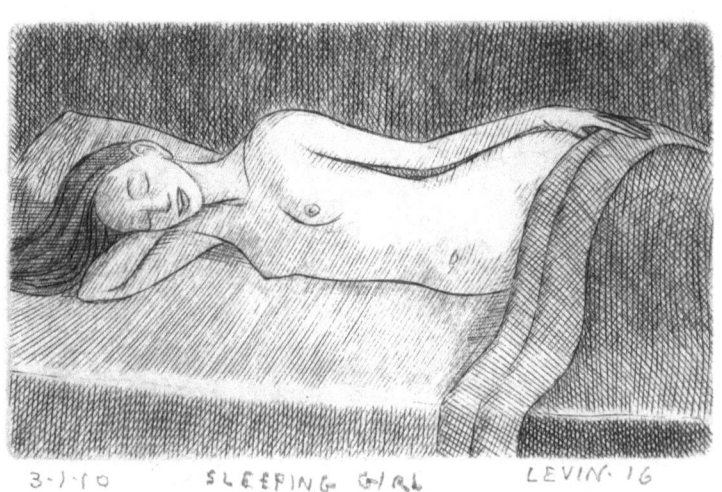

3-1-10   SLEEPING GIRL   LEVIN. 16

Eli Levin
"Sleeping Girl"
Engraving
Dixon, New Mexico USA

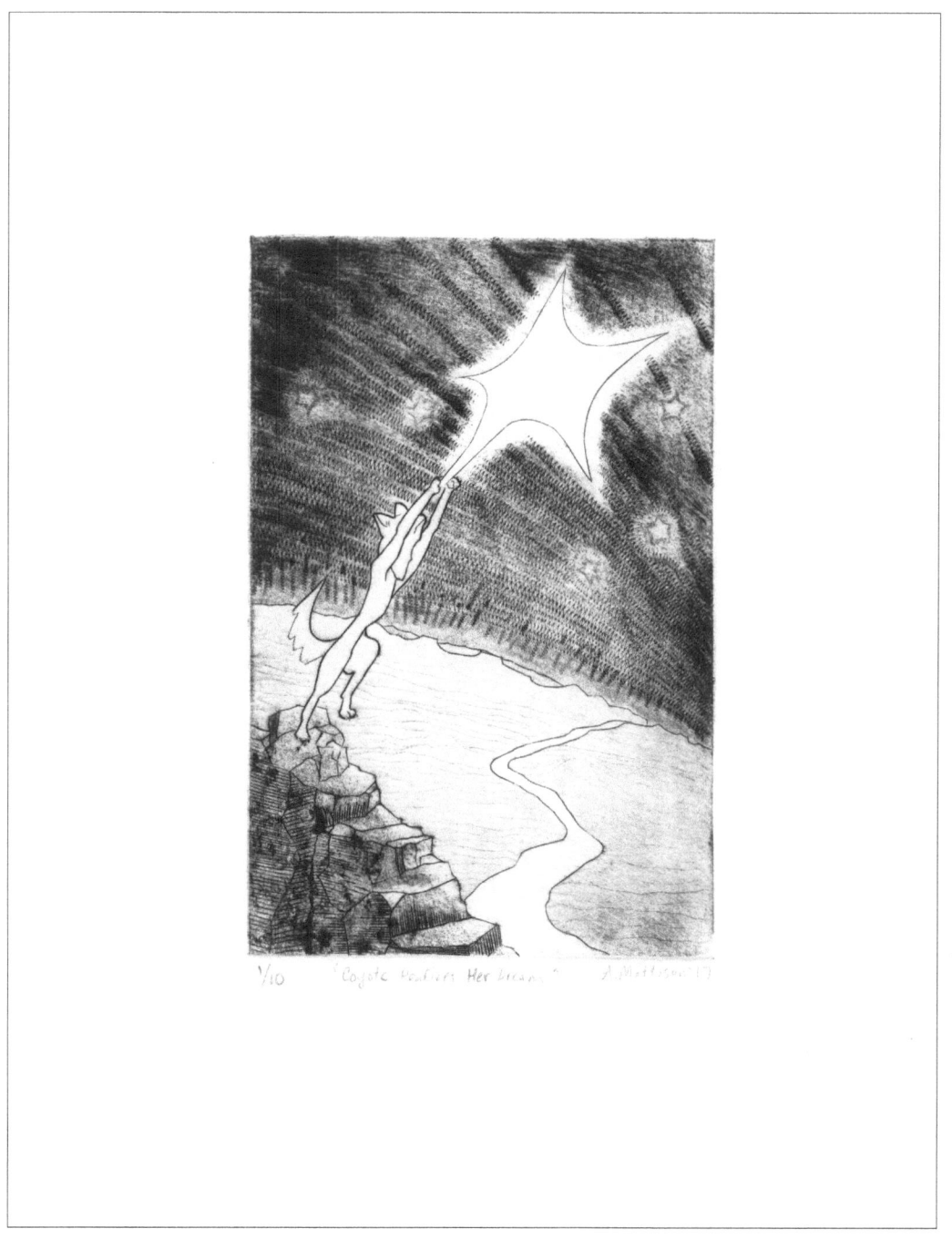

Abby Mattison
"Coyote Realizes Her Dream"
Intaglio
Dixon, New Mexico USA

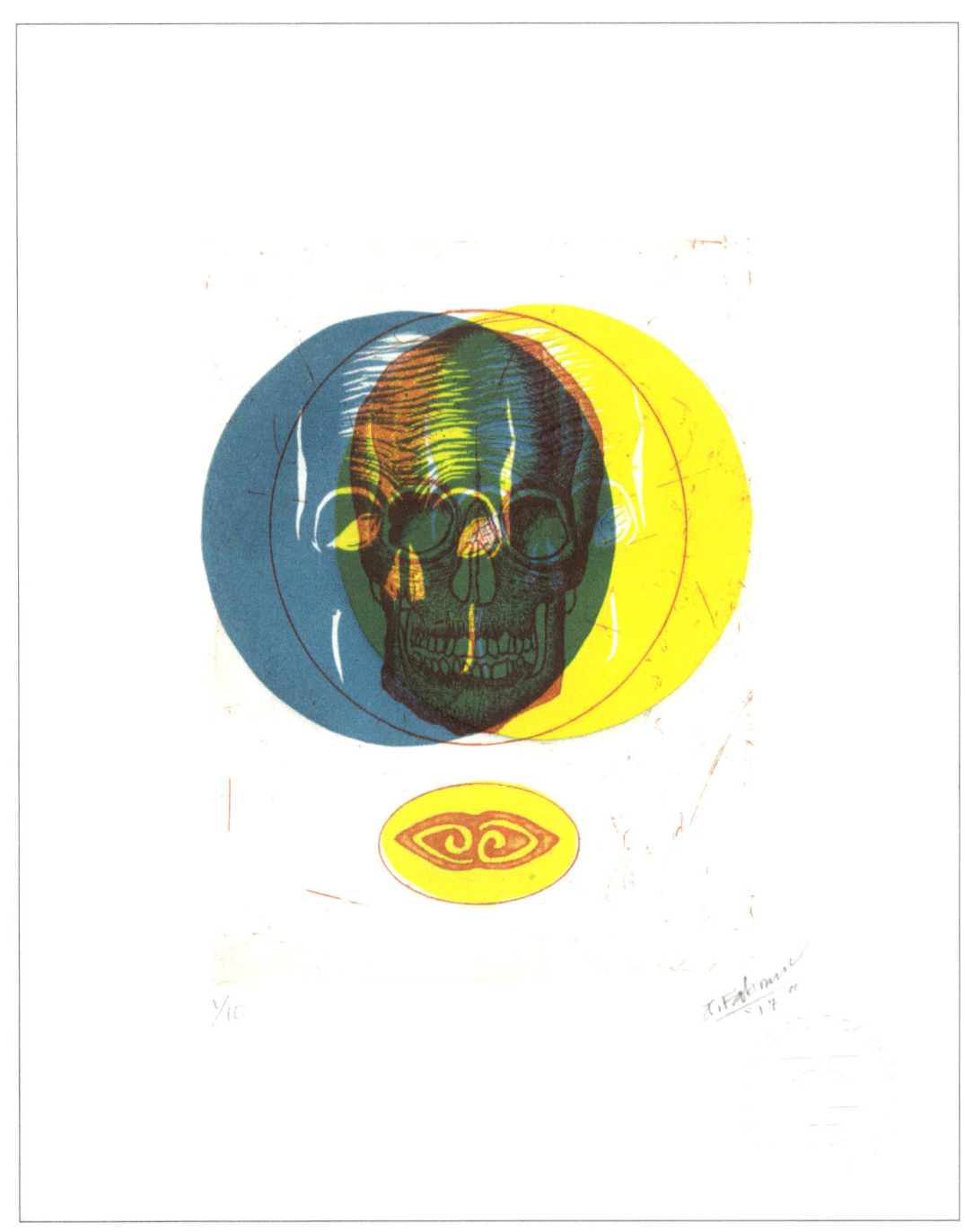

Alberto Fabricio **Melchor** Diaz
Intaglio
Villa de Zaachila, Oaxaca Mexico

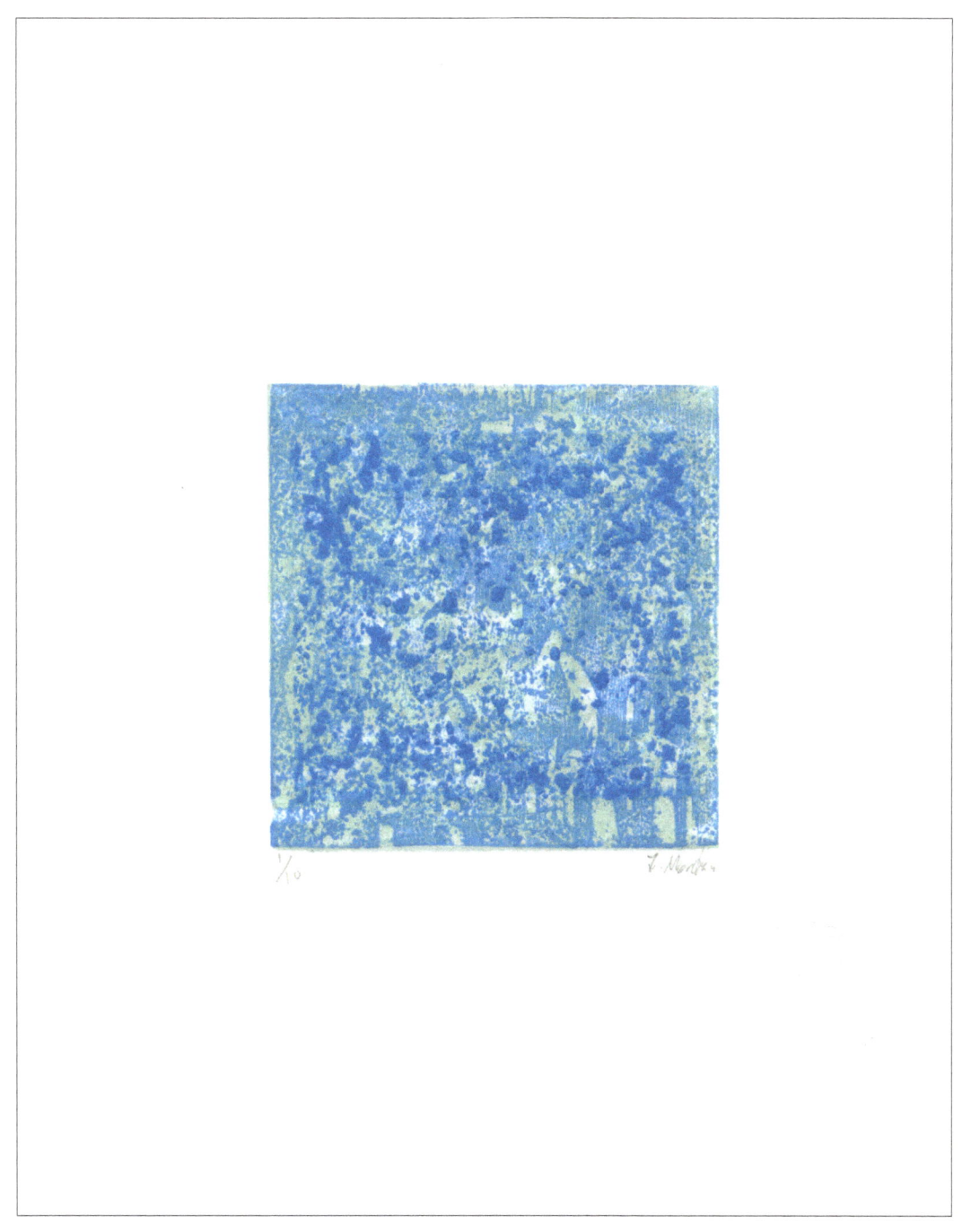

Jorge **Mendoza** Garcia
Collograph
Villa de Zaachila, Oaxaca Mexico

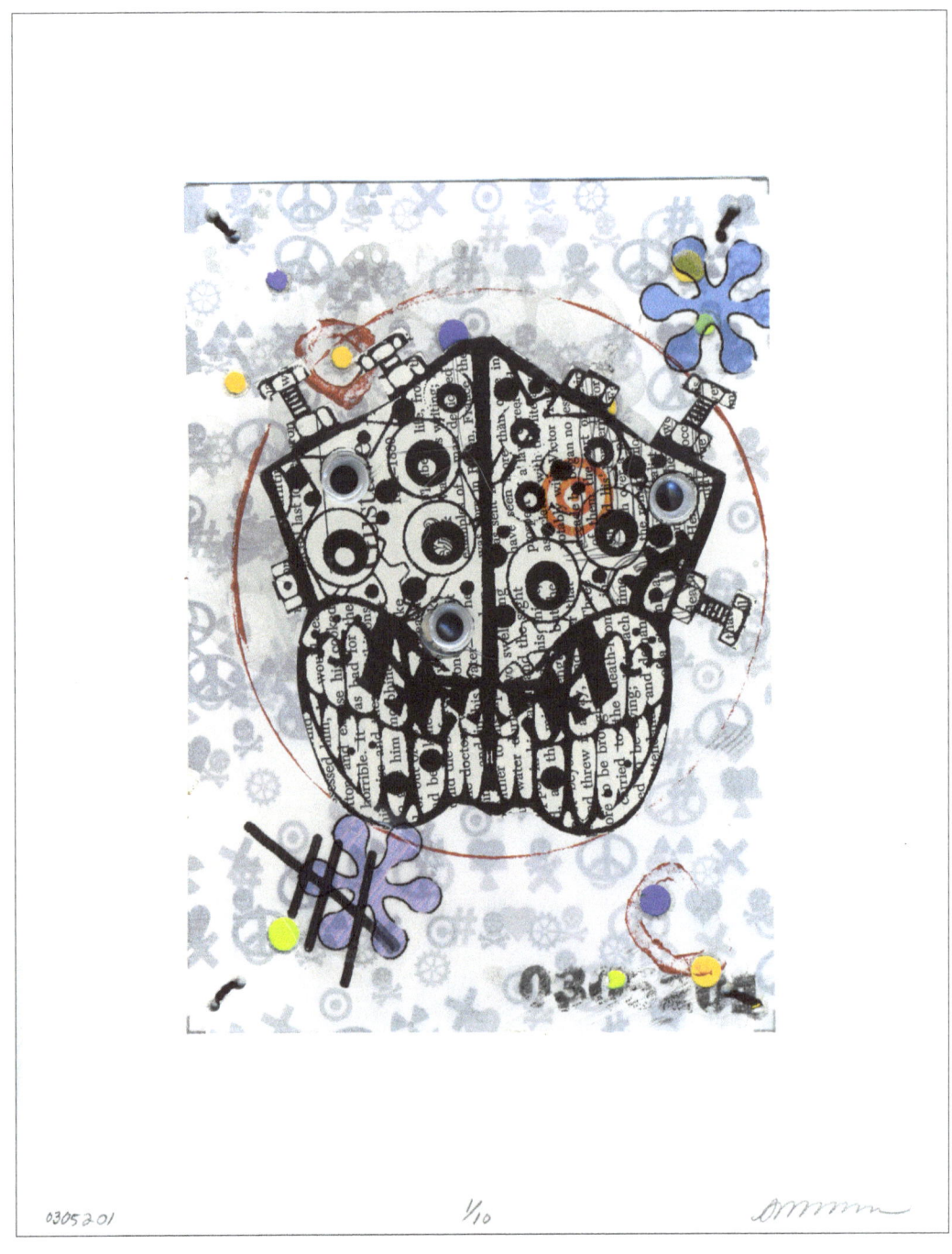

0305201   ¹/₁₀

David **Mohallatee**
"0305201"
Mixed Media
Richmond, Kentucky USA

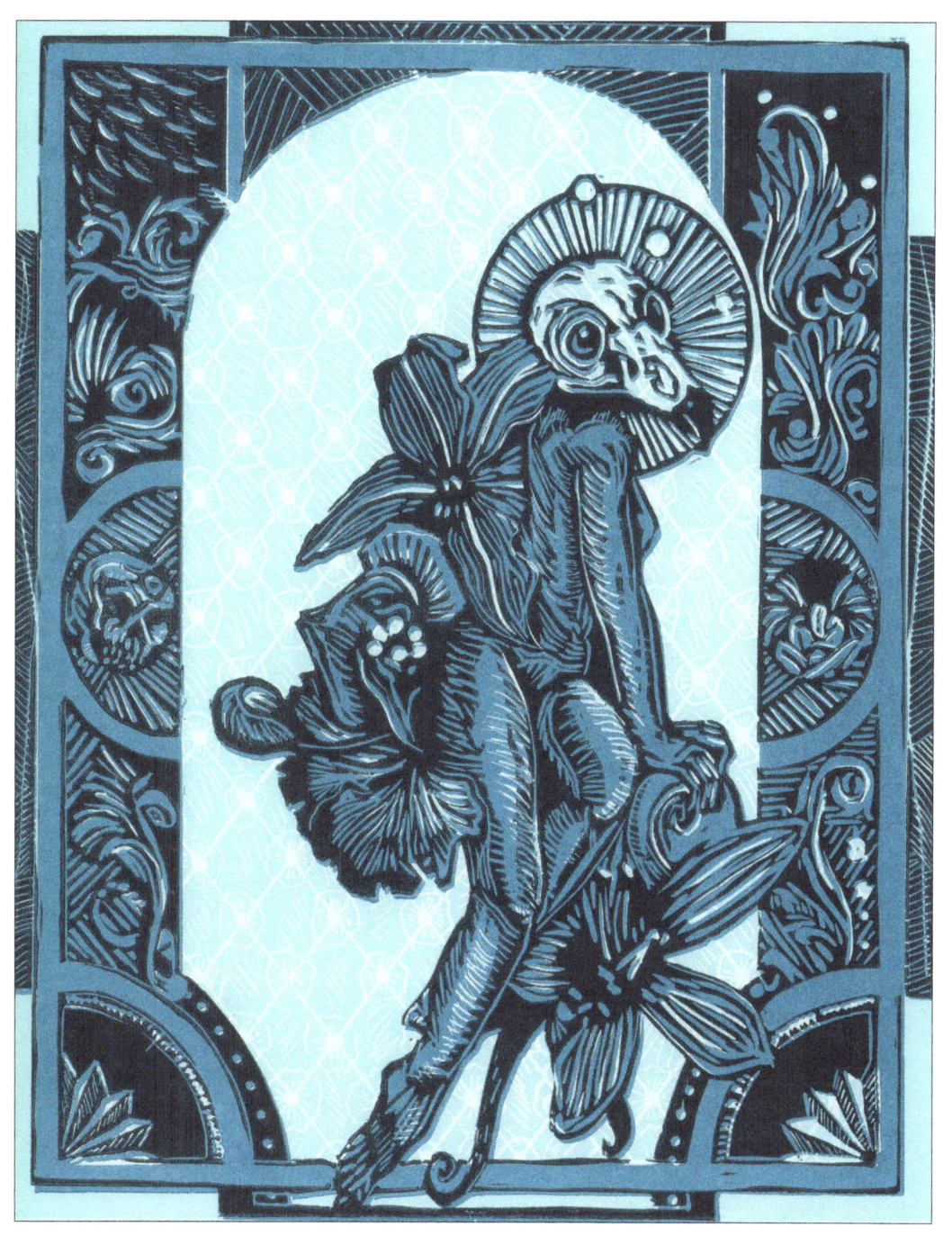

Raul Monarrez
"Estas Como Un Pajarito Muerto"
Relief Print
El Paso, Texas USA

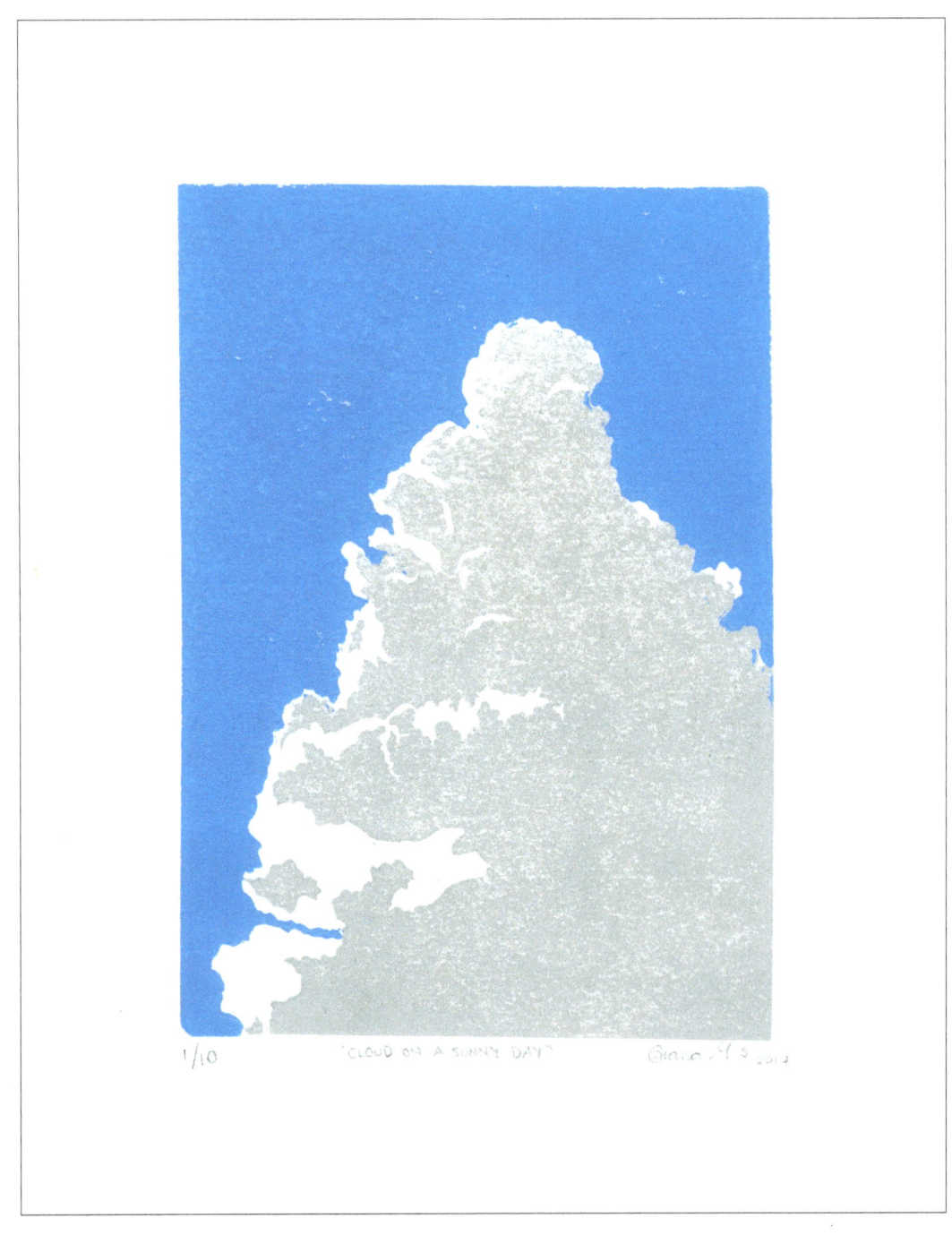

1/10   "CLOUD ON A SUNNY DAY"   Giana M S 2017

Giana Montero
"Cloud On A Sunny Day"
Serigraph
Atherton, California USA

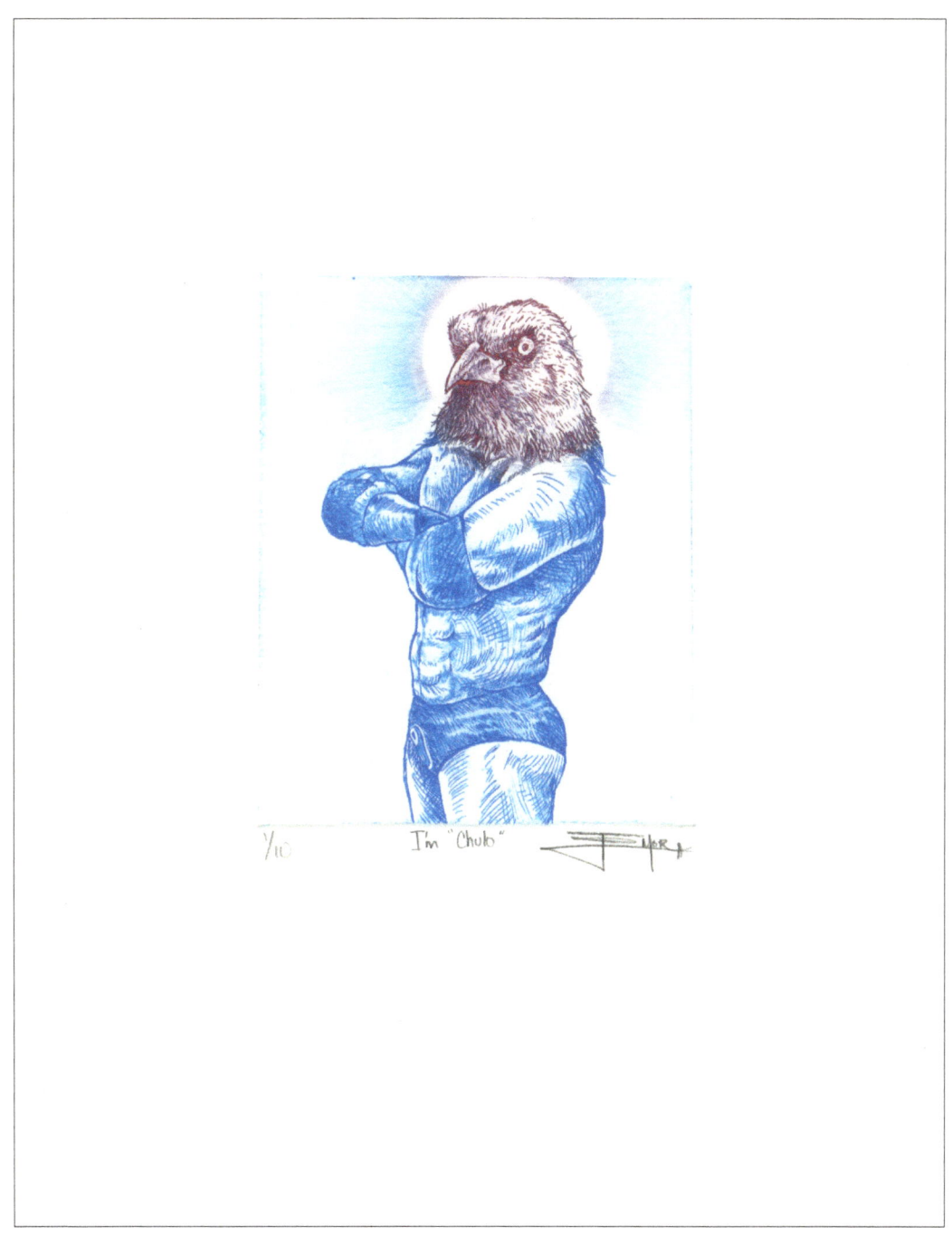

Juan de Dios **Mora**
"I'm Chulo"
Intaglio
San Antonio, Texas USA

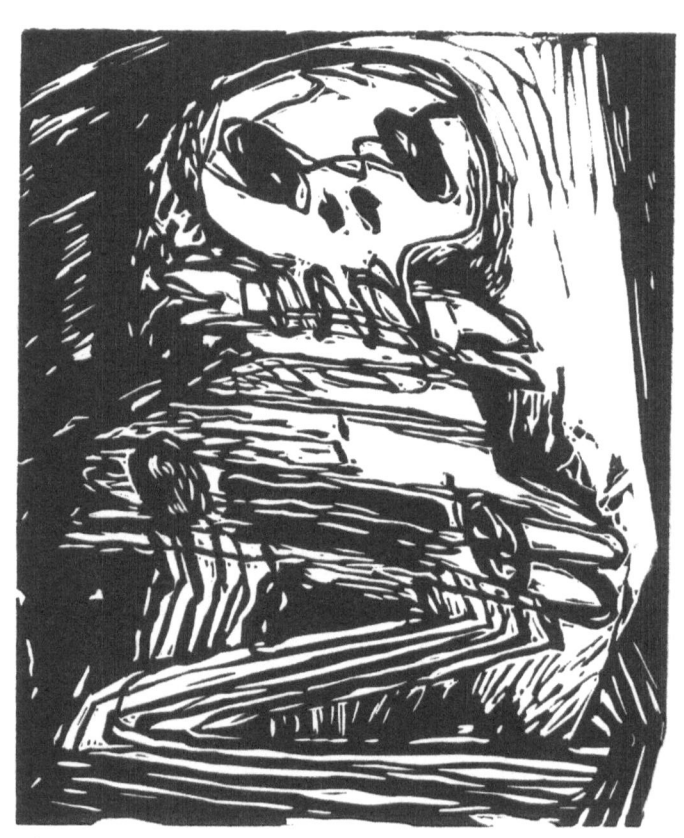

1/10   CARROCERIA   GUSTAVO MORA PEREZ 2017

Gustavo **Mora** Perez
"Carroceria"
Relief Print
Oakland, California USA

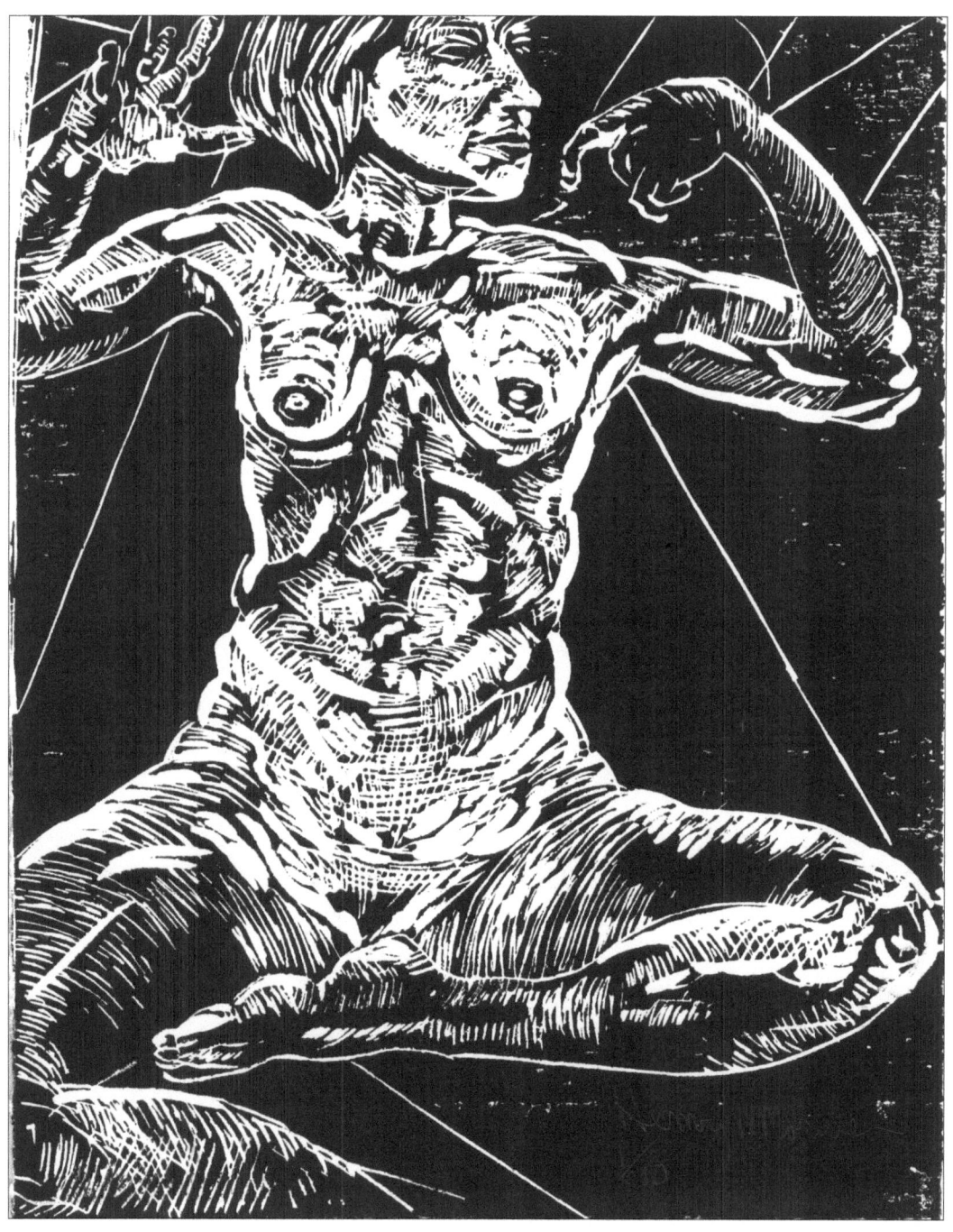

Henry **Morales**
"Nude"
Relief Print
Albuquerque, New Mexico USA

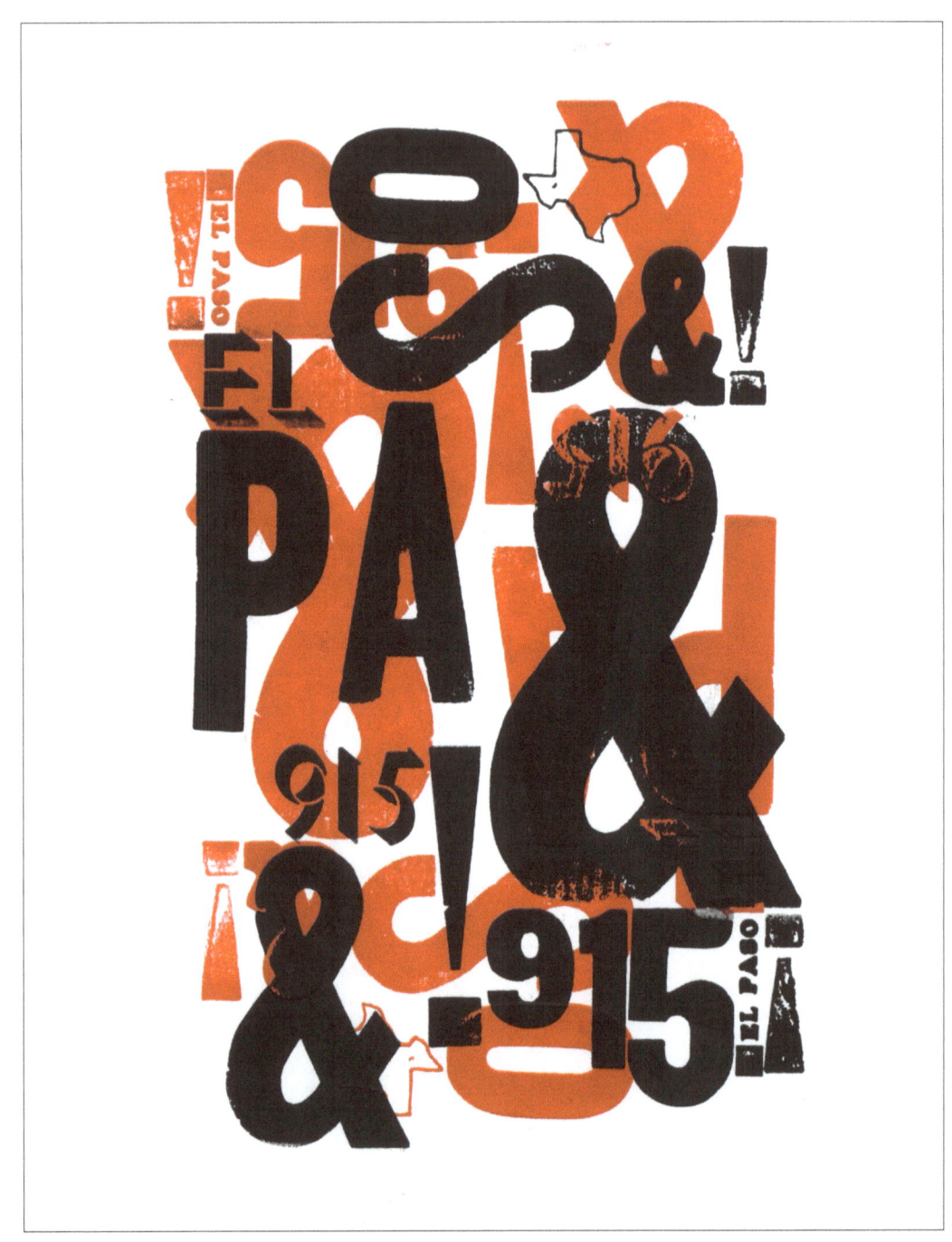

Deena **Mustin**
"El Paso Y Que"
Letterpress
El Paso, Texas USA

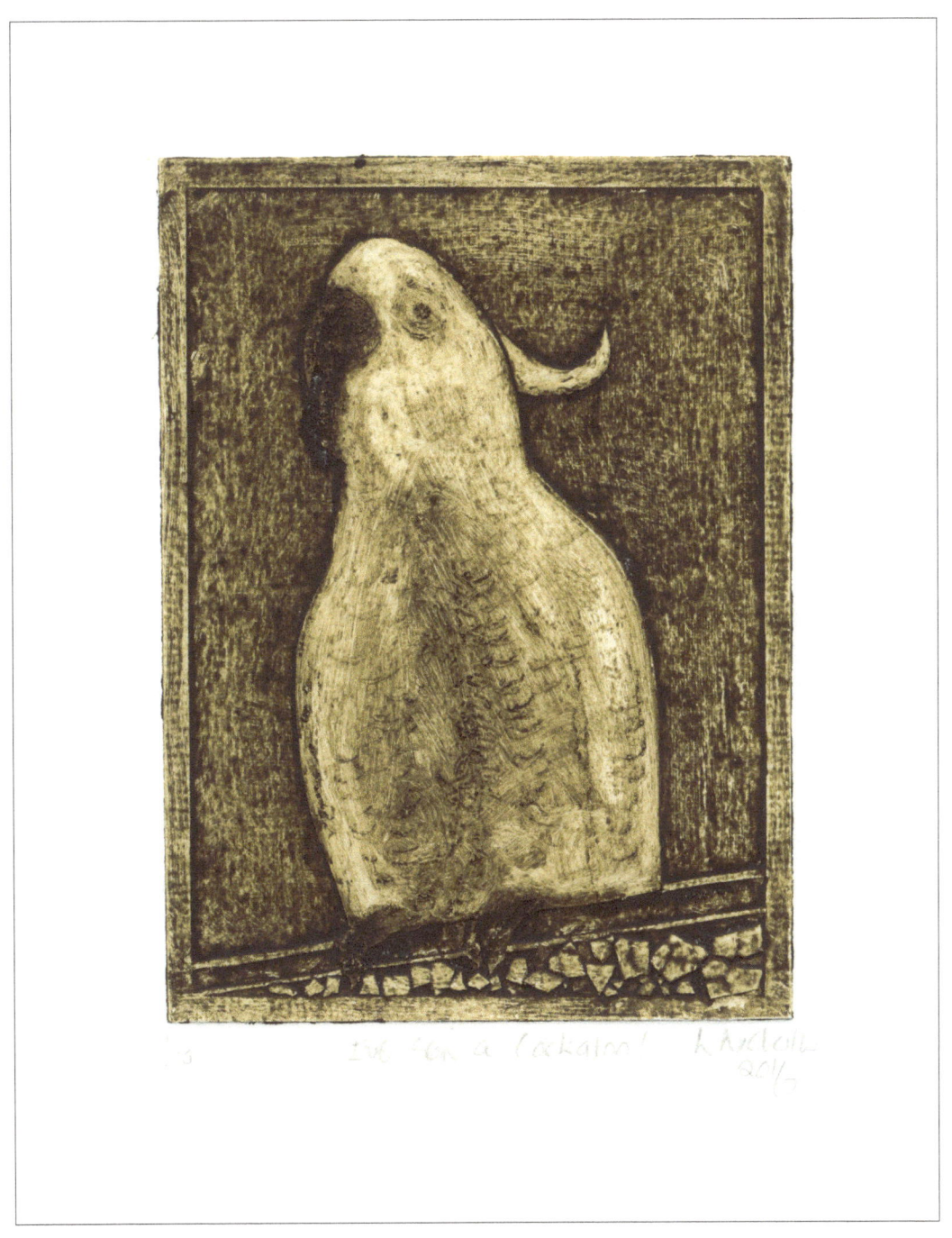

Lyn Nicholls
"I've Seen A Cockatoo"
Collograph
Riddells Creek, Victoria Australia

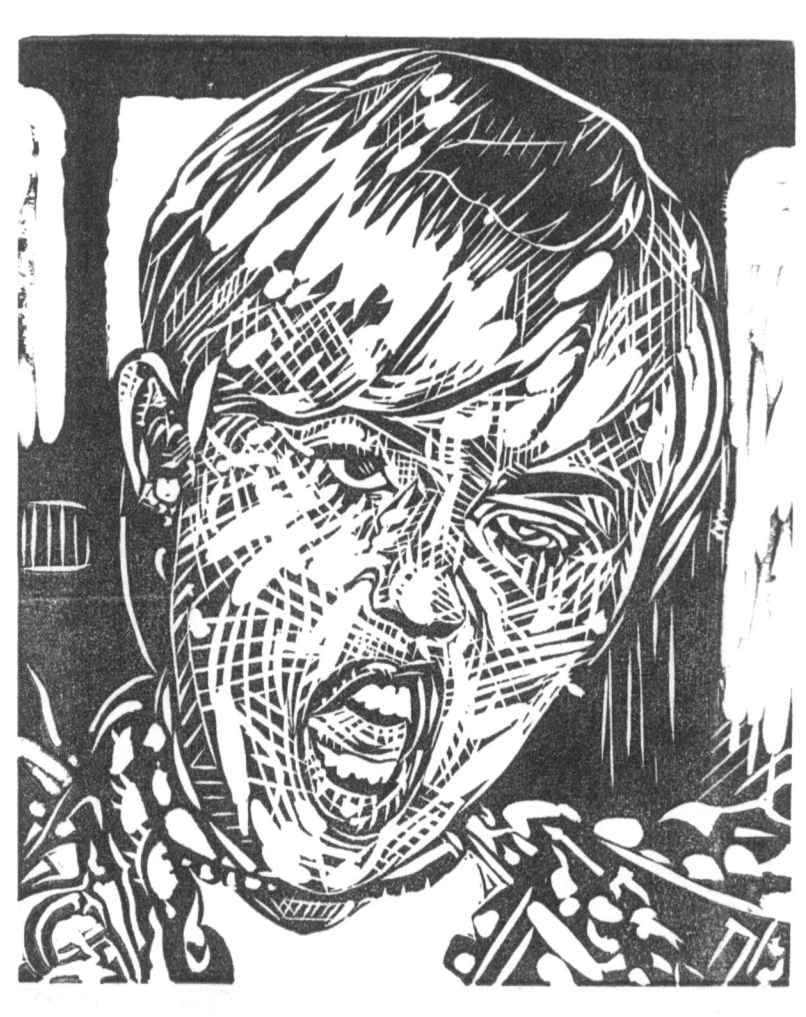

Gabriel Luis **Perez**
"Tear That Cherry Out"
Relief Print
Las Cruces, New Mexico USA

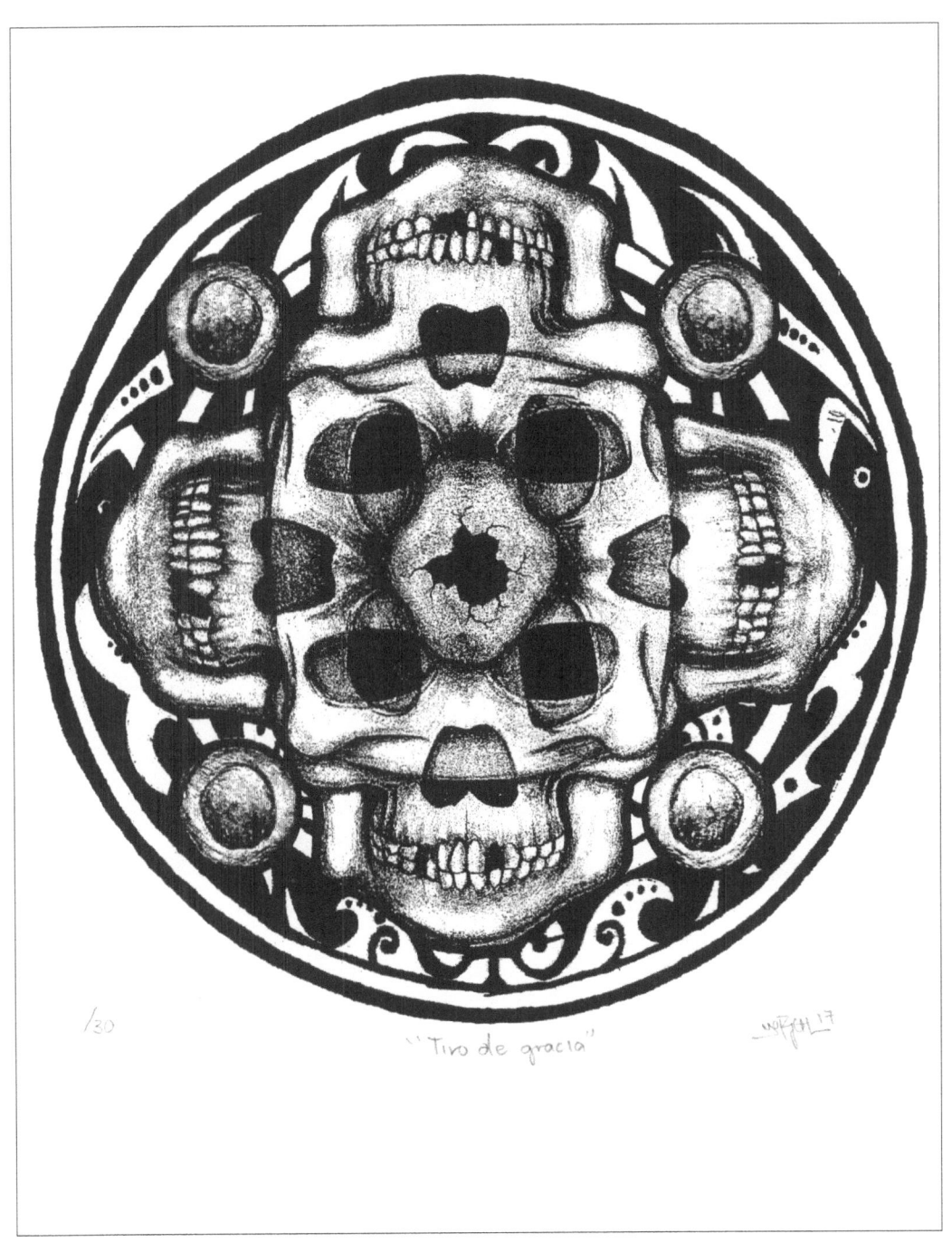

/30

"Tiro de gracia"

Jorge "Yorch" **Perez**
"Tiro De Gracia"
Serigraph
Ciudad Juarez, Chihuahua Mexico

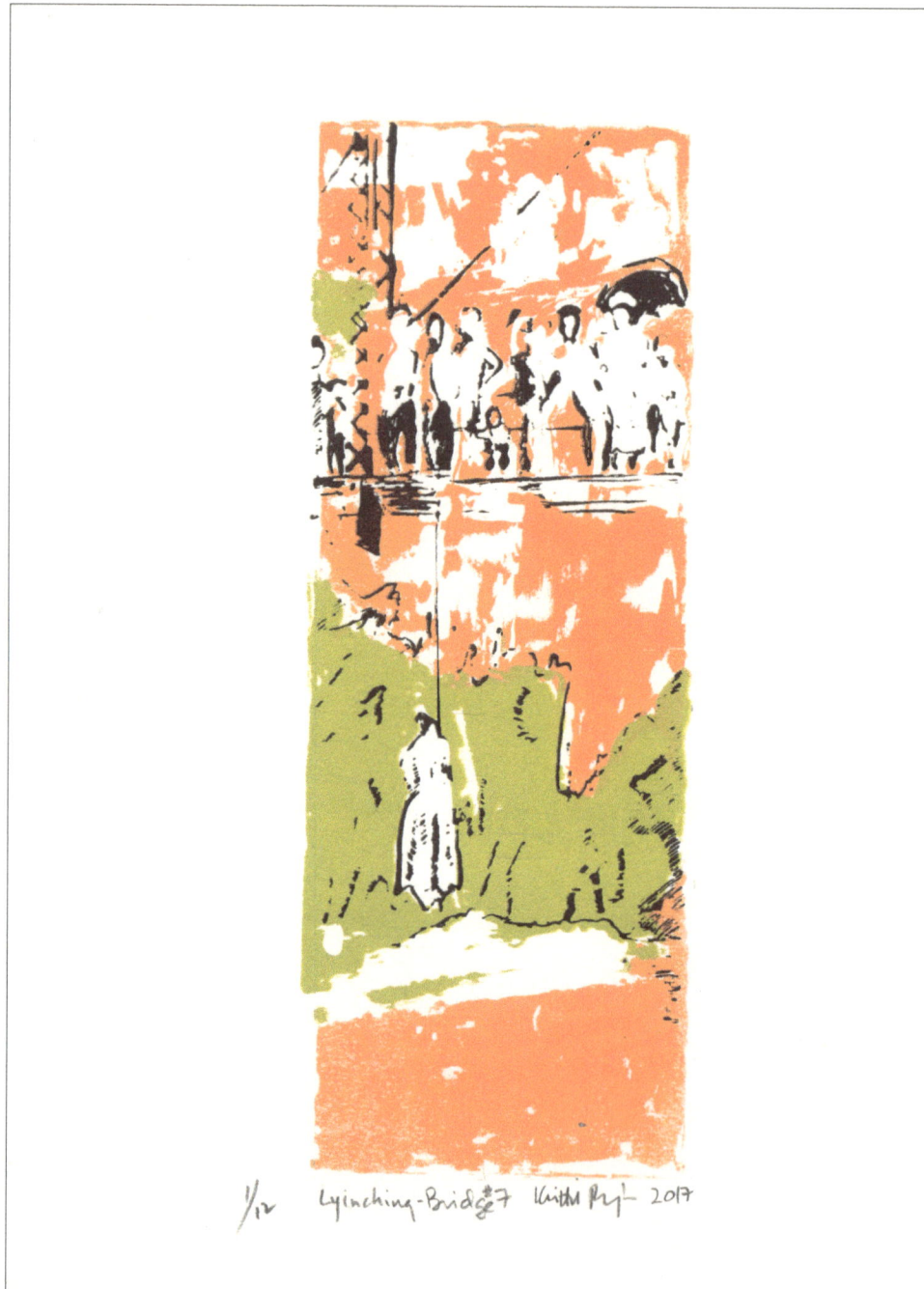

1/12   Lyinching-Bridge #7   Krittika Ryp 2017

Krittika Ramanujan
"Lyinching– Bridge #7"
Serigraph
Albuquerque, New Mexico USA

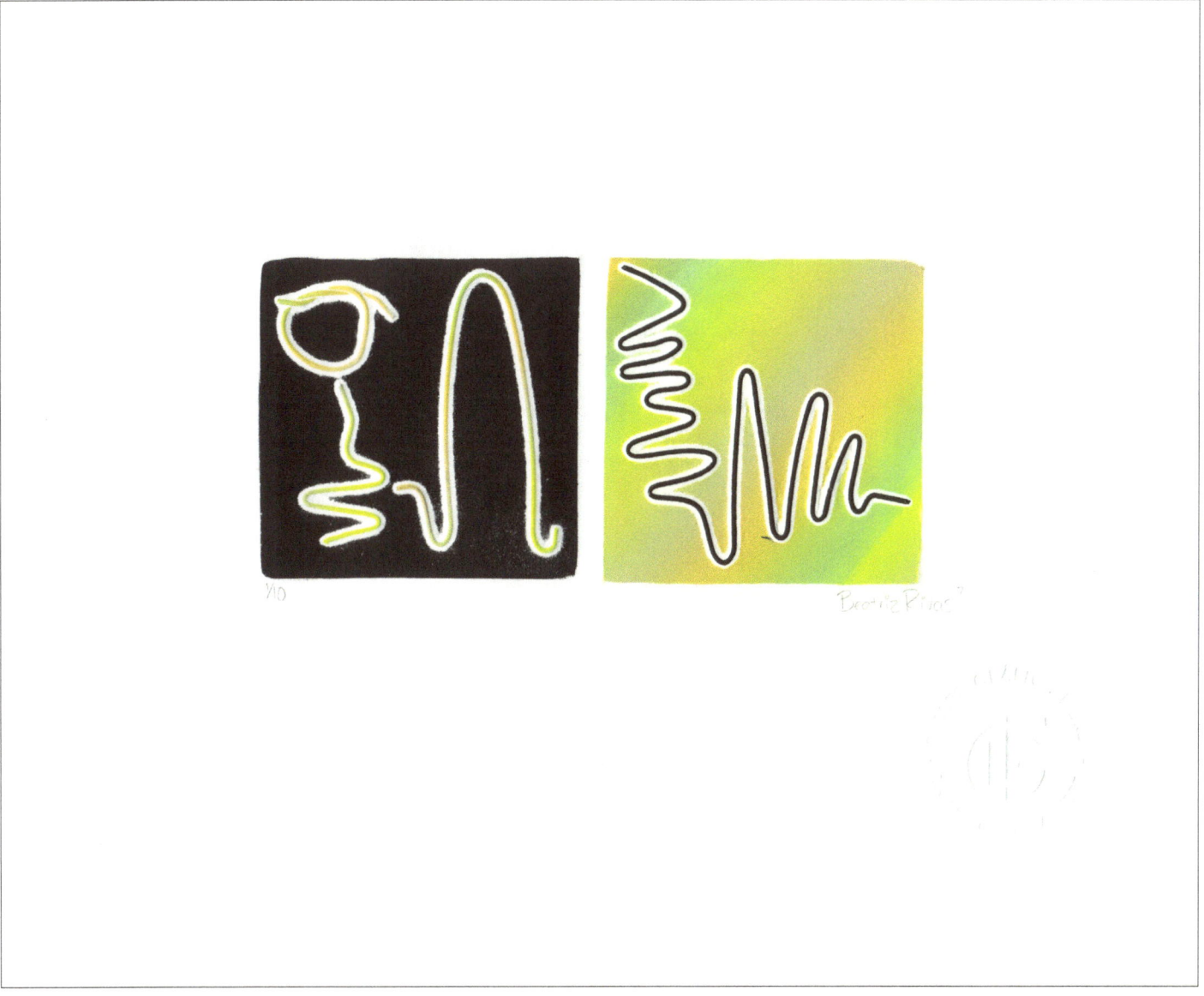

Beatriz A. **Rivas** Palacios
Mixed Media
Villa de Zaachila, Oaxaca Mexico

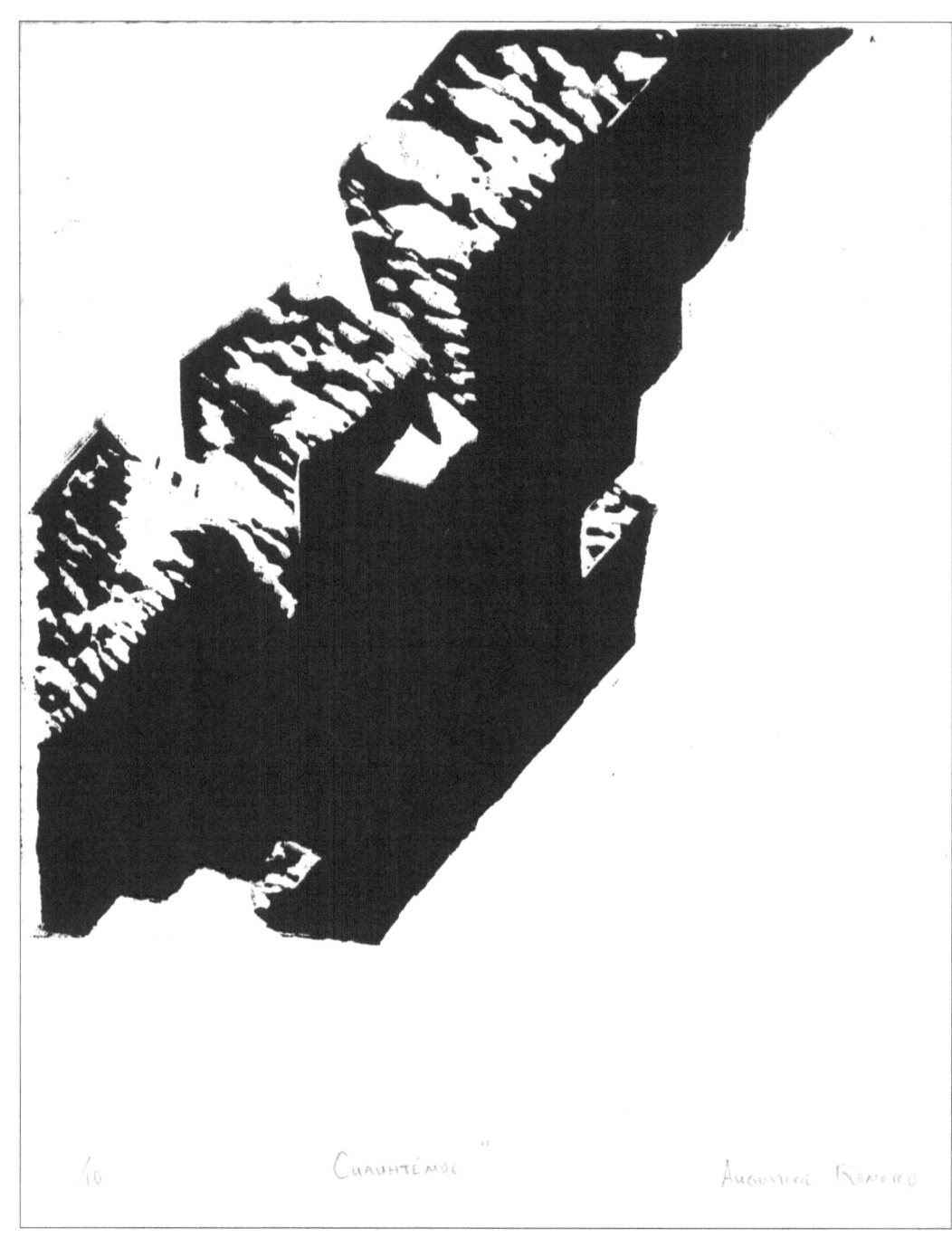

Augustine Romero
"Cuauhtemoc"
Relief Print
Albuquerque, New Mexico USA

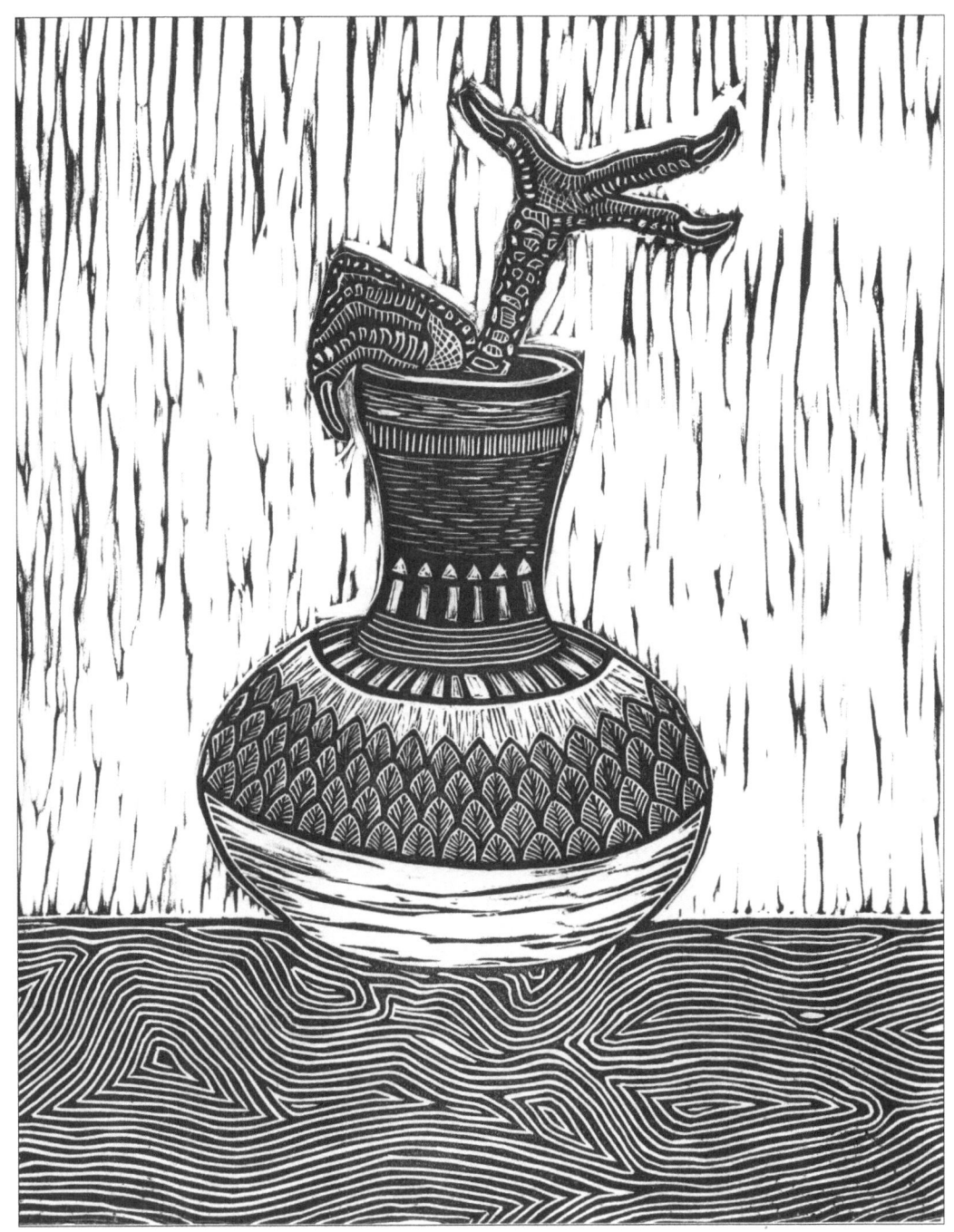

Humberto **Saenz**
"Gallo"
Relief Print
San Antonio, Texas USA

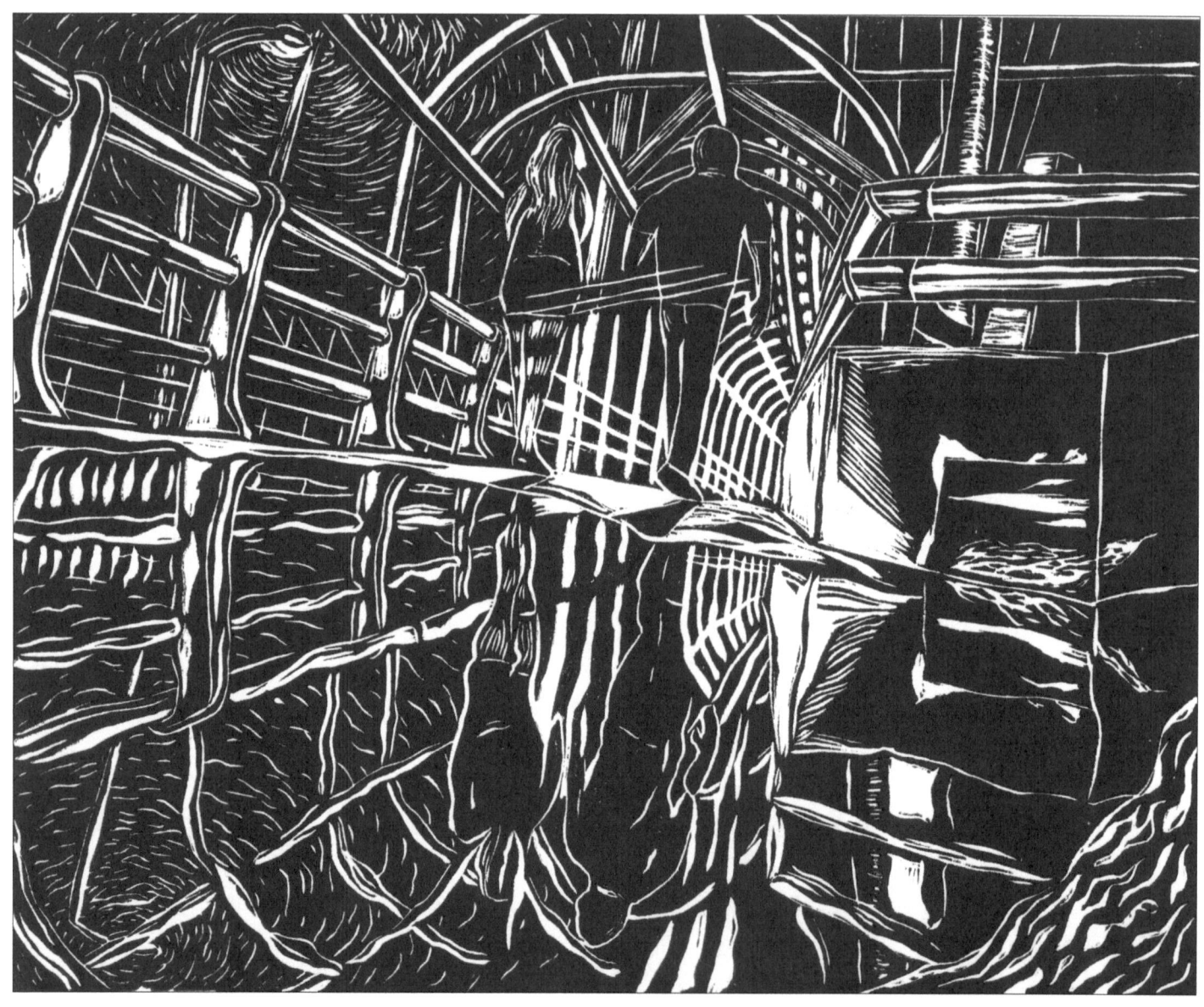

Marco **Sanchez**
"Santa Fe Bridge"
Relief Print
El Paso, Texas USA

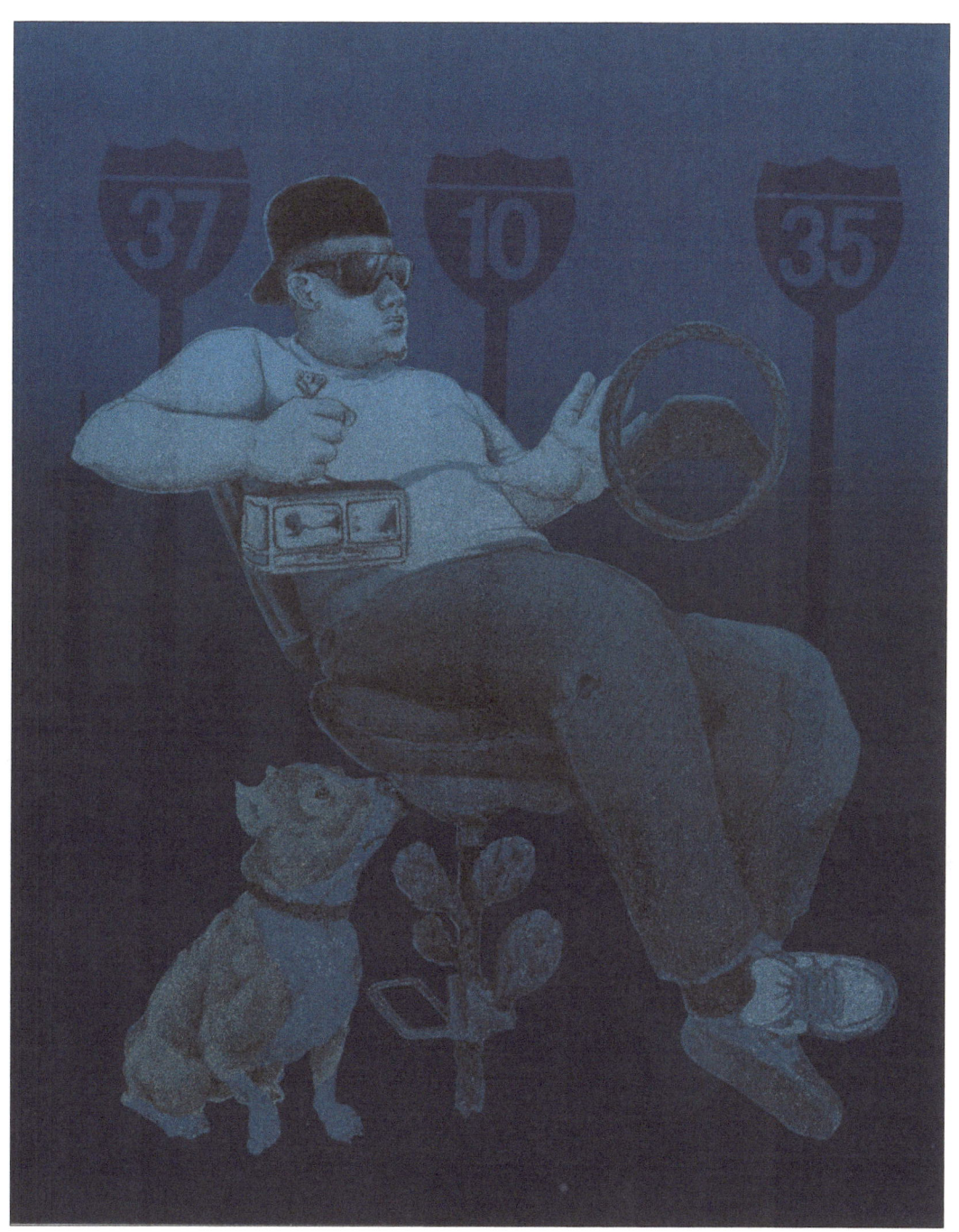

Alan Serna
"Libre Y Luchando"
Lithograph
Lexington, Kentucky USA

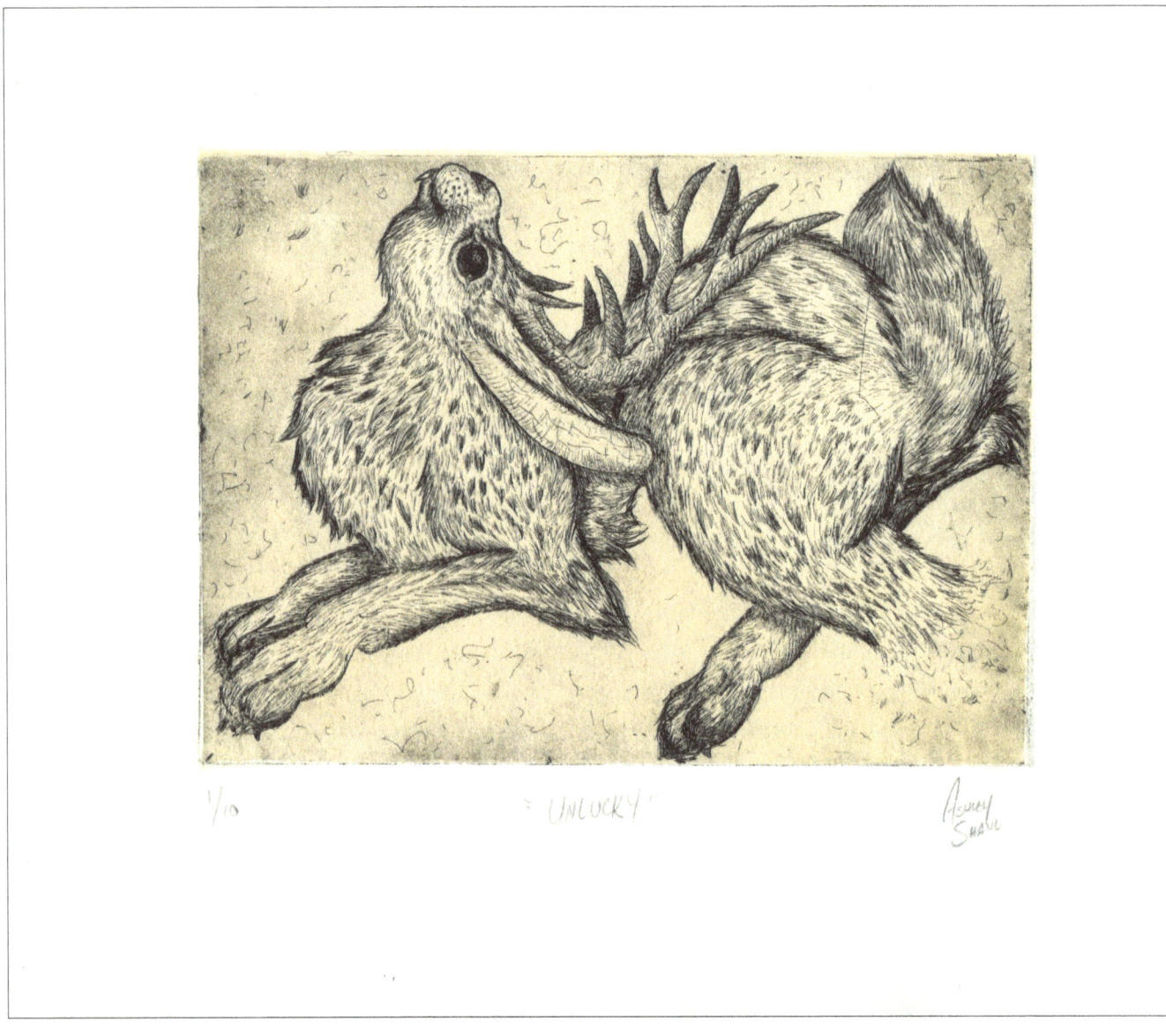

1/10   "UNLUCKY"

Ashley Shaul
"Unlucky"
Intaglio
Eastpointe, Michigan USA

MEMORIES CONVERGE   ⅟₁₀   R STANDER

Ryan Stander
"Memories Converge"
Aquatint
Minot, North Dakota USA

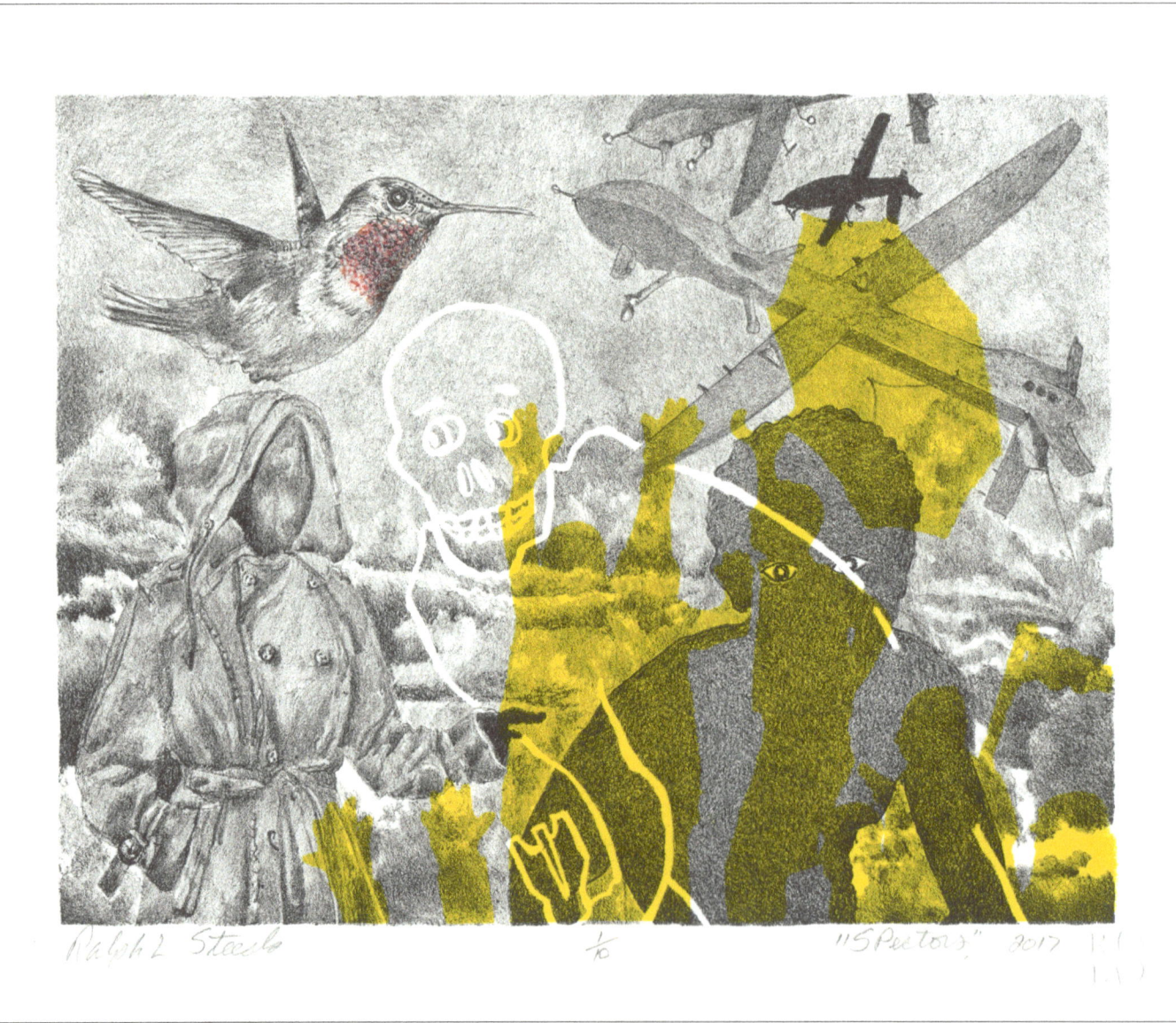

Ralph **Steeds**
"Spectors"
Lithograph
Red Springs, North Carolina USA

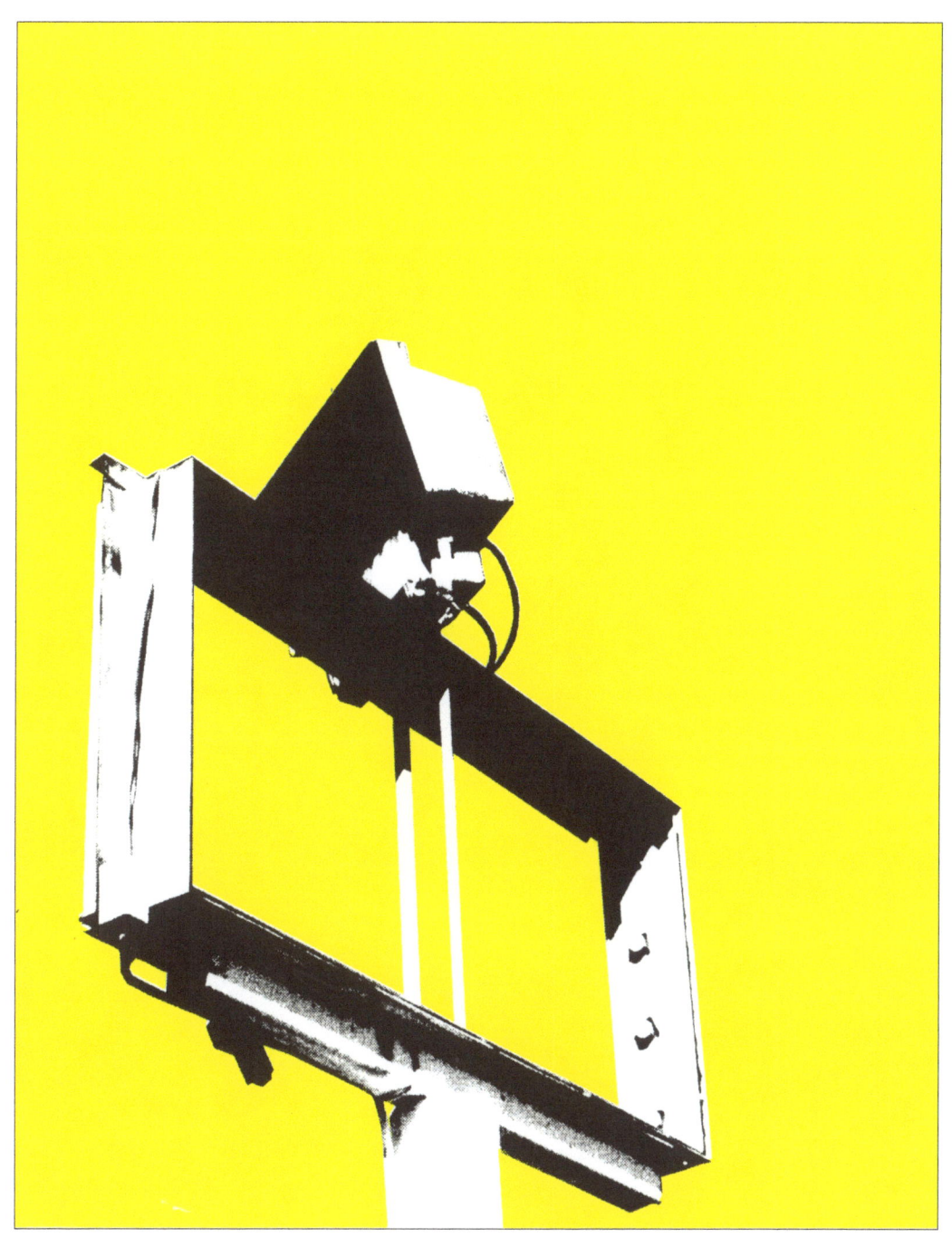

Lorna **Turner**
"Third + North Colorado"
Serigraph
Santa Monica, California USA

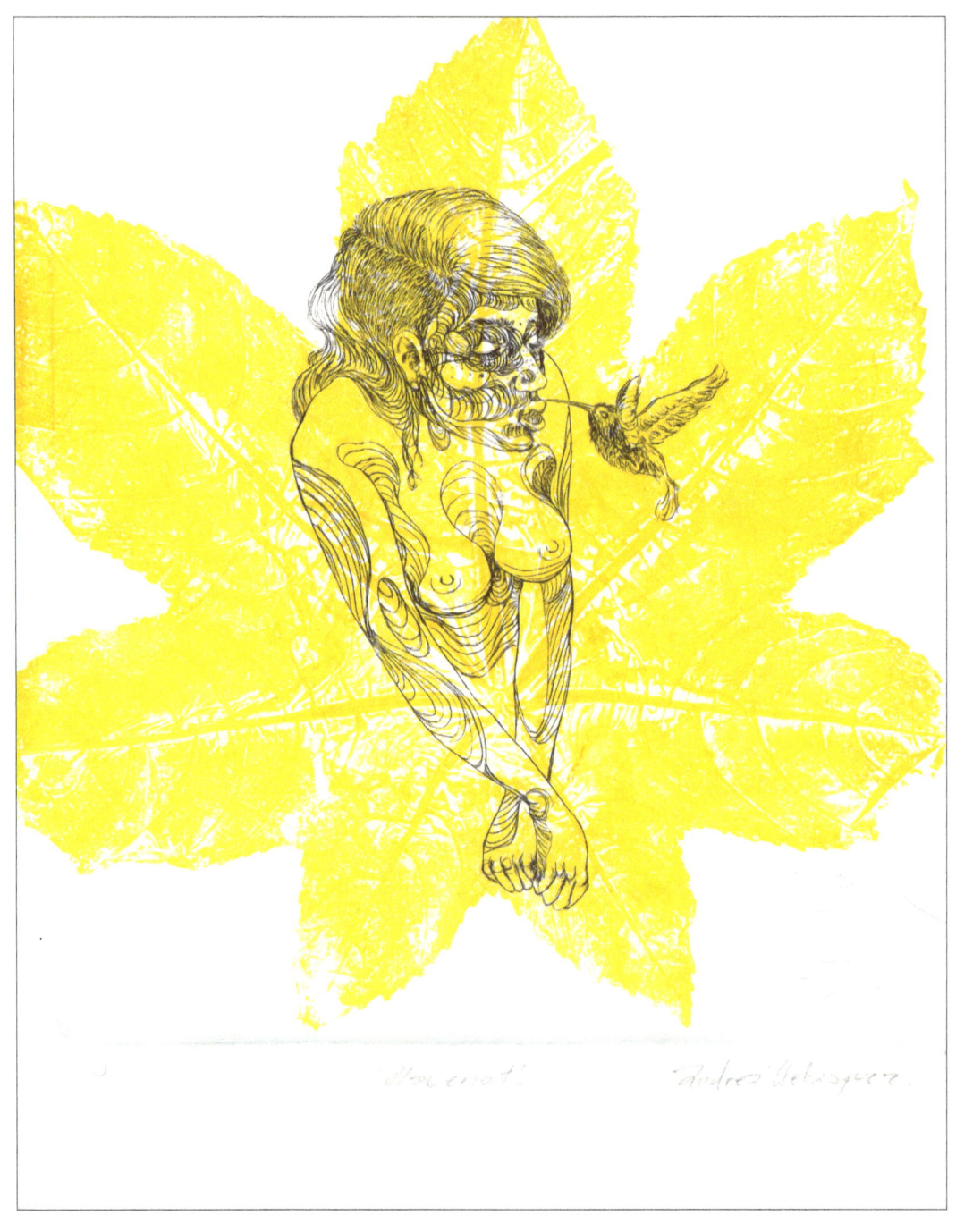

Andrea **Velasquez**
Drypoint/Monoprint
Villa de Zaachila, Oaxaca Mexico

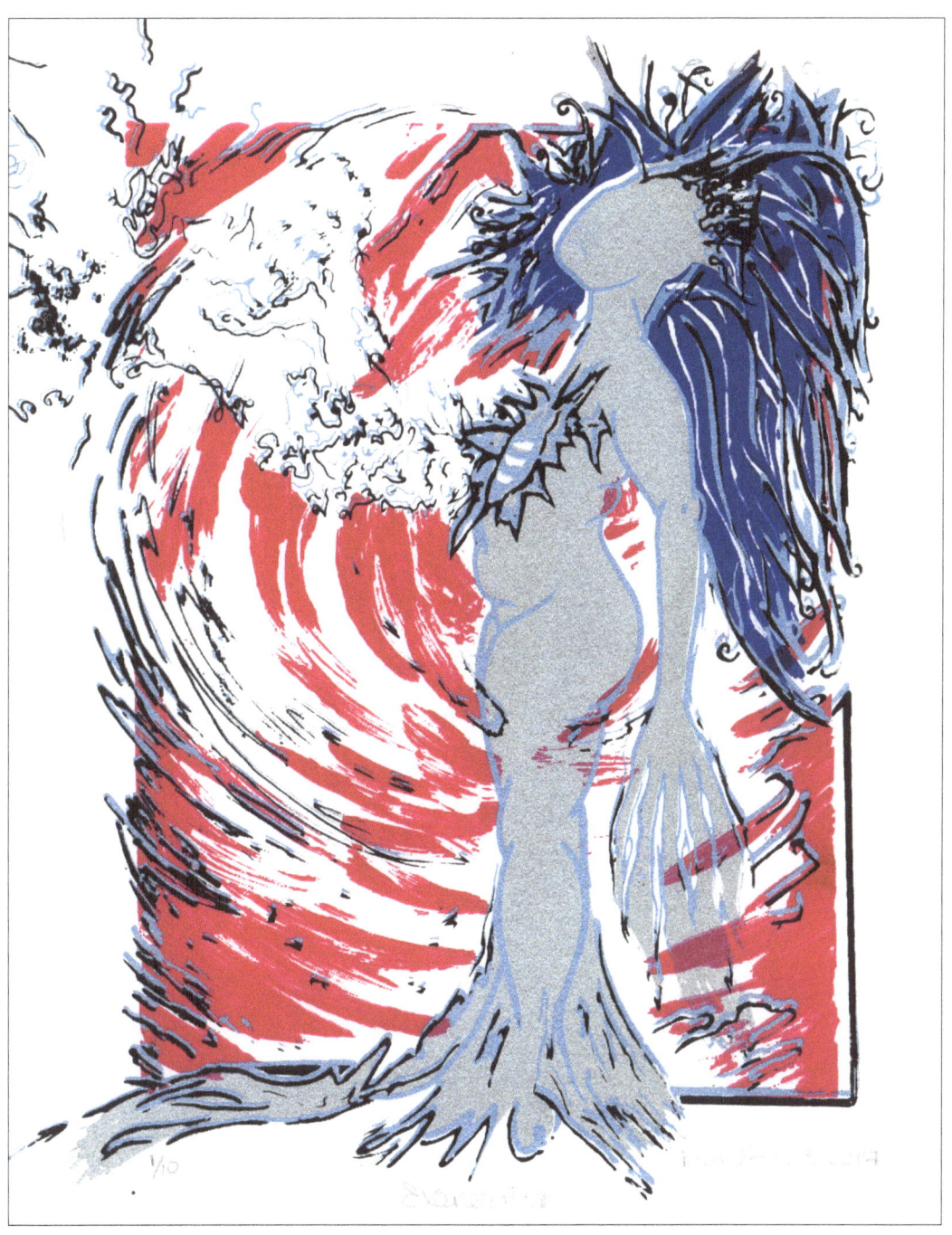

Diane **Vera**
"Exaneration"
Serigraph
El Paso, Texas USA

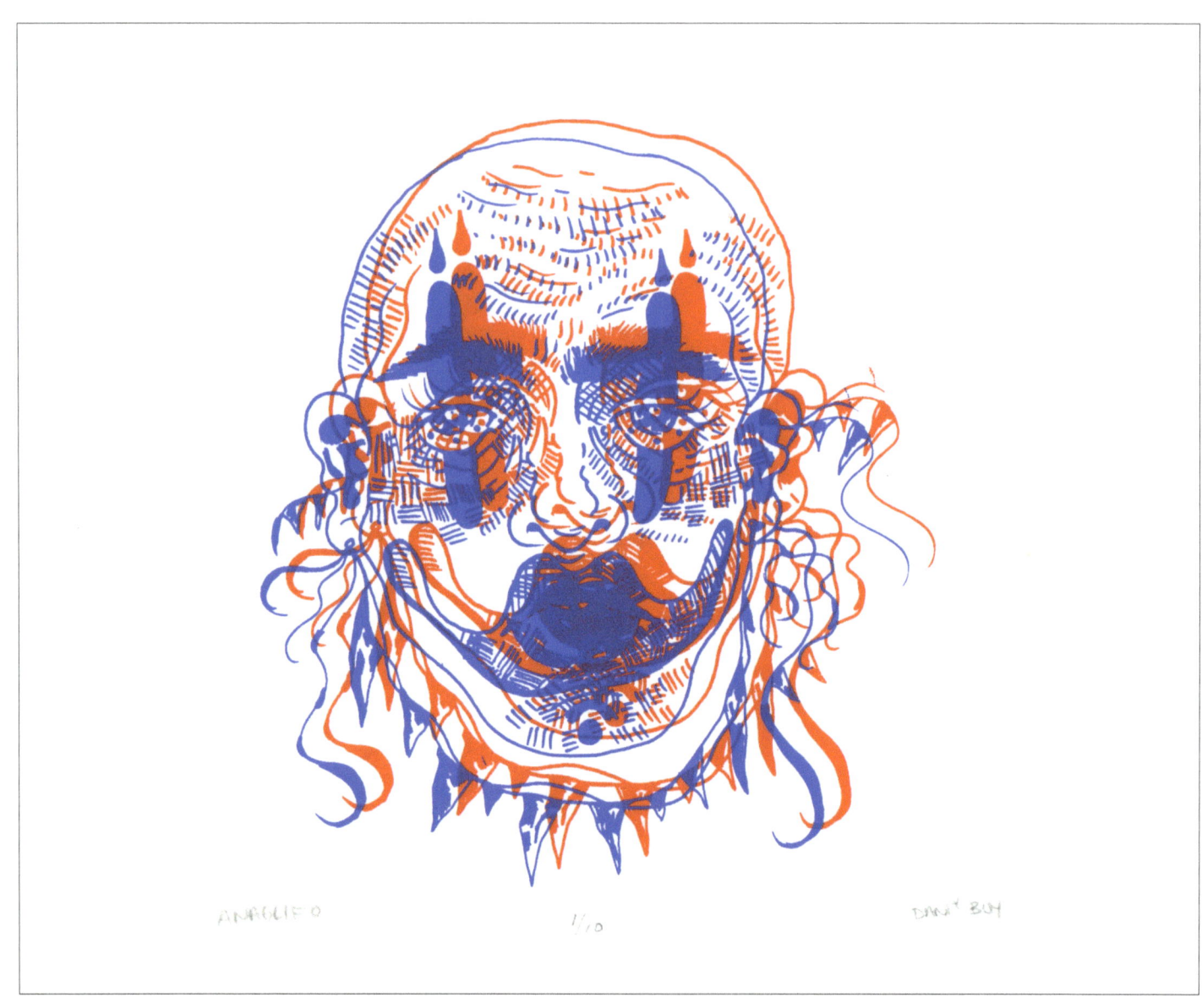

Dania **Villanueva**
"Anaglifo"
Serigraph
El Paso, Texas USA

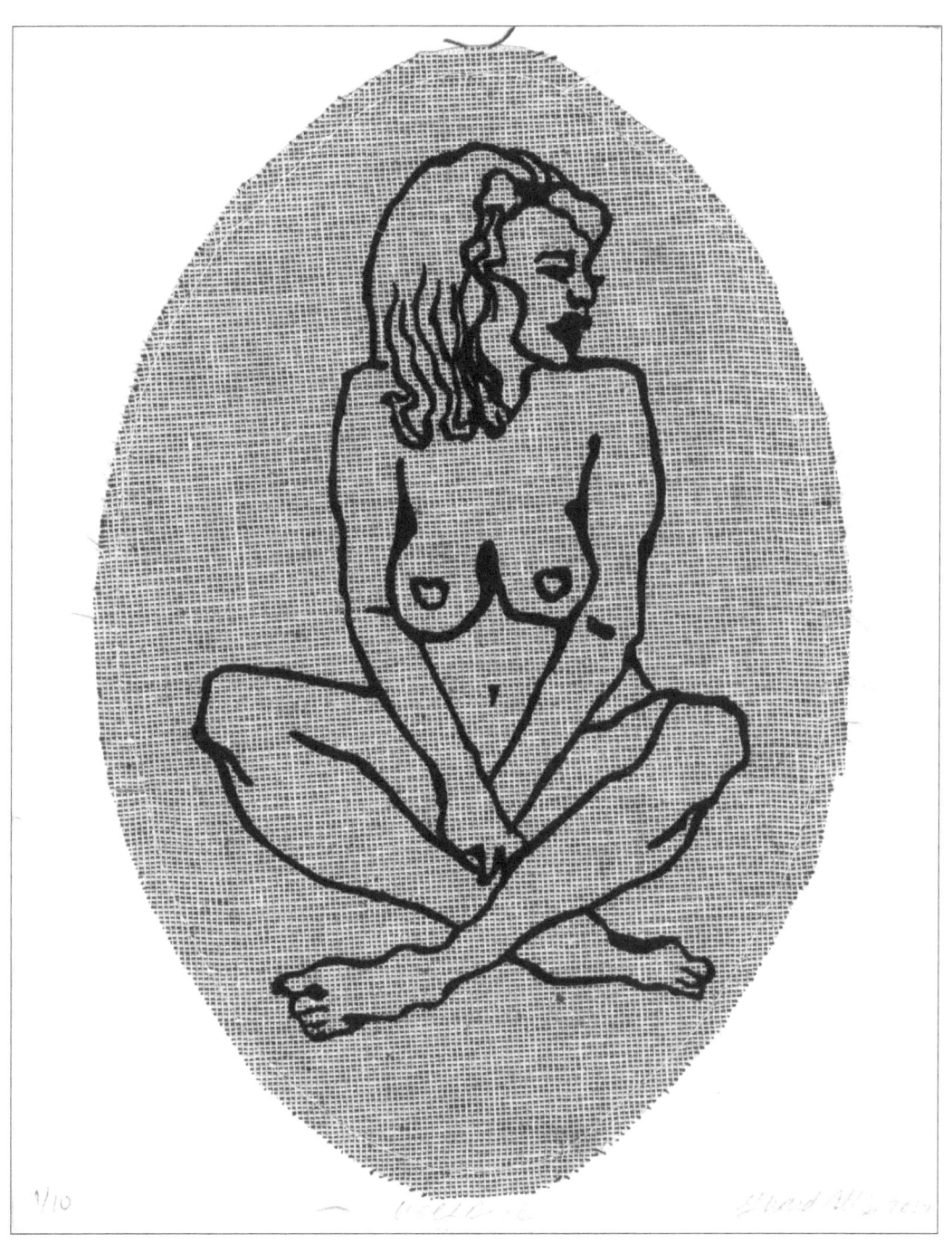

Georgia Ward-Collings
"Wolf Deck"
Serigraph
Seattle, Washington USA

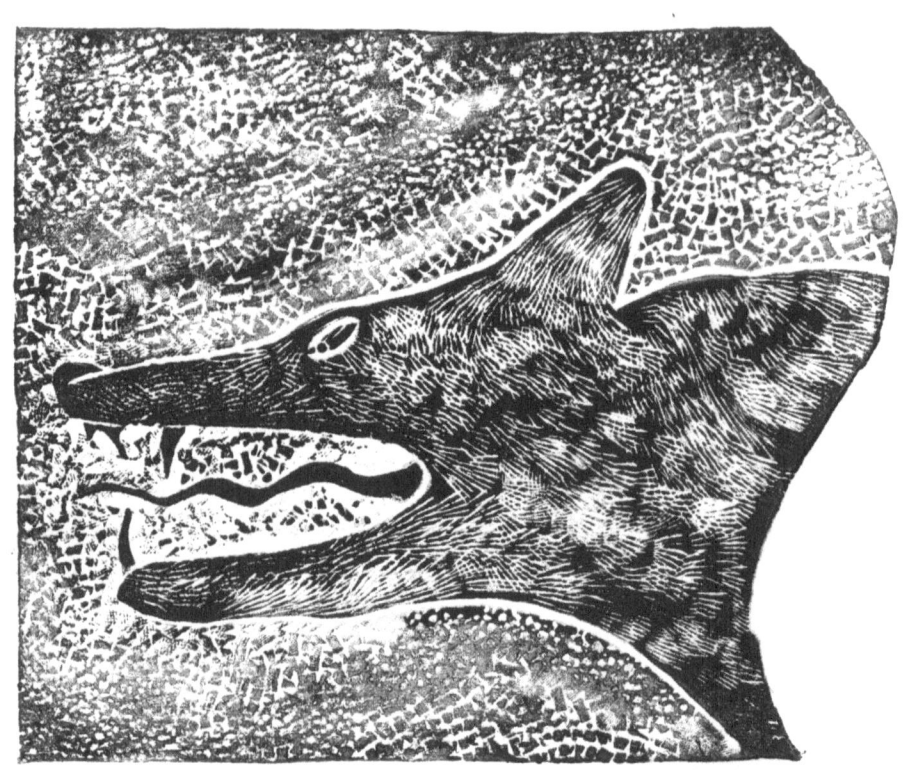

The Wolf's Dog 1/10   Jim Weaver 2017

Jim Weaver
"The Wolf's Dog"
Relief Print
Ada, Oklahoma USA

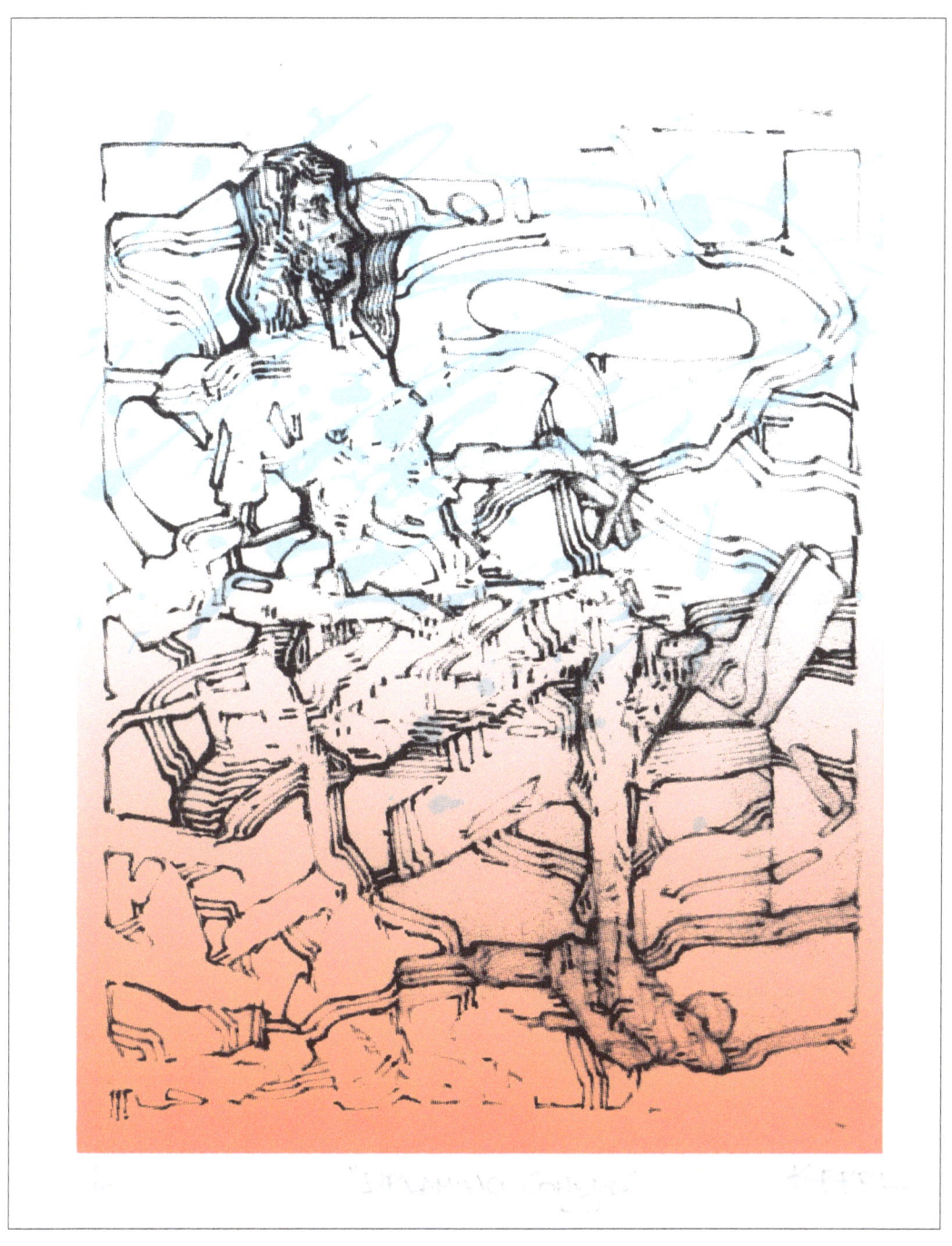

Karl "Krrrl" **Whitaker**
"Dreaming Conejos"
Serigraph
Albuquerque, New Mexico USA

PRINT EXCHANGE II: ARTIST WEB SITES

A

Acevedo, Pavel
*www.facebook.com/
Pages.Pavel.Acevedo*

Aguilar, Miguel

Aguirre, Adrian
tallergraficalibre.wordpress.com

Apodaca, Christin
www.capodaca.com

B

Barista, David

Bass, Aaron
www.crowsfootpress.com

Beauchamp, Louise
www.louisebeauchamp.co.uk

Brown, Laurie D.
lauriedbrown.com/biog.html

Buack, Glenn
www.facebook.com/glenn.buack

C

Cranney, Ashley B.
*arizonaprintgroup.com/artists/
ashley-cranney*

D

Davis, Diane
www.dianecdavis.com

deGruyter, Aaron
www.aarondegruyter.com

Delgado, *Francisco
franciscodelgado.weebly.com*

Doering, Maria
www.maria-doering.com

F

Felix Martinez, Hector Josue

Flores, Miguel

Floss, Jules
julesfloss.com

G

Garcia, Sam

Gonzalez, Susan "Skuishi"
www.instagram.com/skuishiii

Gray, Cameron
www.facebook.com/MREverClear

Guerra, Manuel
www.manuelguerra.net

H

Hodgins, Eric
erichodginsstudio.blogspot.com

L

Lane, Brian
www.printzerostudios.com

Levin, Eli
*argos-gallery.com/Argos_Site/
jo_eli_gallery1.htm*

M

Mattison, Abby

Melchor Diaz, Alberto Fabricio

Mendoza Garcia, Jorge

Mohallatee, David
www.davidmohallatee.com

Monarrez, Raul
*deserttriangle.blogspot.com/
2015/08/raul-monarrez.html*

Montero, Giana

Mora, Juan de Dios
www.facebook.com/juan5mora

Mora Perez, Gustavo
www.gustavomora.net

Morales, Henry
*deserttriangle.blogspot.com/
2015/10/henry-morales.html*

Mustin, Deena
*www.theproperprintshop.com/
products/deena-mustin*

N

Nicholls, Lyn
*printmakersnow.wordpress.
com/2017/03/14/
artist-interview-lyn-nicholls*

P

Perez, Gabriel Luis
gabrielluisperez.com

Perez, Jorge "Yorch"
*www.youtube.com/
watch?v=vR64ALHreds*

R

Ramanujan, Krittika
www.krittikar.com

Rivas Palacios, Beatriz A.
tallergraficalibre.wordpress.com

Romero, Augustine

S

Saenz, Humberto
www.humbertosaenz.com

Sanchez, Marco
*thefusionmag.com/fusion-
gallery-marco-sanchez*

Serna, Alan
www.alanserna.com

Shaul, Ashley
www.ashleyshaul.com

Stander, Ryan
www.ryanstander.com

Steeds, Ralph
www.ralphlsteeds.com

T

Turner, Lorna
www.smallchop.com

V

Velasquez, Andrea
*museodemujeres.com/
en/news/397-exposicion-
de-mujeres-grabadoras*

Vera, Diane
dianevera.weebly.com

Villanueva, Dania

W

Ward-Collings, Georgia
georgiawardcollings.weebly.com

Weaver, Jim
www.jww-art.com

Whitaker, Karl "Krrrl"
krrrl.blogspot.com

NUMBER OF ARTISTS BY COUNTRY/STATE

Texas – 13

New Mexico – 9

California – 5

Arizona – 4

Washington – 4

Kentucky – 2

Illinois – 1

Michigan – 1

Missouri – 1

North Carolina – 1

North Dakota – 1

Oklahoma – 1

Mexico – 7

Canada – 1

UK – 1

Australia – 1

www.ingramcontent.com/pod-product-compliance
Lightning Source LLC
Chambersburg PA
CBHW051048180526
45172CB00002B/556